D1327066

Britain

Britain

A Guide to Architectural Styles
from 1066
to the
Present Day

•••

Hubert
Pragnell

A CIP record for this book is available from the British Library

Published by •••ellipsis, 2 Rufus Street, London N1 6PE
http://www.ellipsis.com
Designed by Jonathan Moberly

First edition 1995
Second (updated) edition 1999
Copyright © 1999 Ellipsis London Limited

ISBN 1 84166 002 7

Printed and bound in Hong Kong

•••ellipsis is a trademark of Ellipsis London Limited
For a catalogue or information on special-quantity orders
of Ellipsis books please contact us on0171–739 3157 or
sales@ellipsis.co.uk

Contents

DEDICATION

To
Dorothea, who accepts that for me architecture is more important than a hot meal
Charlotte, who sympathises with her mother when I rush off to look at a building
and Christian, who likes Canary Wharf and anything taller

Introduction

We can learn much about a period of history from the study of architecture, particularly when little in the way of written evidence or other visual artefacts survives. A church represents the spiritual aspirations of a local community; a cathedral may show the results of endowments by clergy, nobility and even pilgrims who came to pray at the shrine of a saint. Some may display evidence of royal favour with chantry chapels and lavish tombs. Houses come in many forms, from the humble cottage to the mansion of a nobleman. For obvious reasons the former is likely to be insubstantial and easily destroyed by man or nature. The latter might have played a part in the diplomatic and social power struggle between families aspiring to royal or political favour, or asserting the simple maxim that wealth demands size.

This book cannot claim to be comprehensive in coverage, but presents nevertheless a broad outline of the main phases of architectural development from the Norman Conquest to the present day. Styles overlap in period and, like fashions, often seem to go round in circles. So we have medieval Gothic and nineteenth-century Gothic; or eighteenth-century Queen Anne and early twentieth-century revival. Building materials also vary from region to region: flint churches are common in eastern England but not in the north; half-timbered cottages are common in Kent and Sussex but not in Derbyshire; brick or stone-clad warehouses of the nineteenth century are a feature of large ports and industrial centres but not of the south-coast resorts.

Frequently the history of architecture features only the finest examples of architectural development, especially so in the field of domestic building. Oxburgh Hall, Norfolk, is romantic, constructed in pinkish brick and adorned with battlemented turrets and ornamented chimneys; however the near contemporary cruck cottage in Didbrook, Gloucestershire, also has a place in the story of architecture. The formal grandeur of Bath or the Gothic villas of north Oxford have immediate appeal, but there is much to be observed in the variety of terraced house from the later nineteenth-century suburb.

As the story arrives at the present century so the movements and examples become so numerous that it is impossible to allow more than a brief mention or passing reference. My choice of examples must therefore be selective. However, because of their significance in the development of architecture in the seventeenth century I have devoted separate chapters to Jones and Wren. In the case of the latter, whose contribution to the rebuilding of post-fire London was considerable, my choice of examples must be limited and drawings even more so. It is often necessary to represent a building from several angles in order to convey a true impression. Occasionally a drawing may have an advantage over a photograph in that detail can be emphasised, or the drawing may comprise several different viewpoints.

As with a study of the history of painting, the best experience is to study in front of the actual example. A good reproduction of Monet's *Thames at Westminster* (1870) may look impressive, but to visit the National Gallery is to see the picture in a totally fresh light. The paintwork is alive. To visit Barry and Pugin's Houses of Parliament gives one a feel of size and drama unobtainable from pictures. Only by visiting Canterbury Cathedral can we let it take us over as the magic of ancient stonework speaks to us.

We must also remember that a building, whether it be a cathedral, parish church, or country house may have only assumed its present appearance during recent decades. A cathedral or parish church serves the needs of a community in praise of God and may have grown to accommodate an increasing population, or increasing numbers of pilgrims, or may have been expanded through endowments to accommodate a family burial. A great house might have gone through several major reconstructions or expansions in its history. It might have a medieval core, yet eighteenth-century living rooms and a nineteenth-century library, all set within seventeenth-century walls. So a house may be basically Jacobean on the outside but Adam or even Gothic inside.

In which period do we place a building? This question often faces the restorer, whether it be English Heritage at the Queen's House, Greenwich, or the National Trust at Chastleton, Oxfordshire, or those currently engaged in restoring the apartments damaged by fire at Windsor Castle. The study of a specific building can thus be a challenge and the exact sequence of development not at all easy to follow, not least when there have been stylistic revivals.

This book is written as an invitation to go out and explore. We are after all fortunate in having an architectural heritage which dates back through many centuries and spreads the length and breadth of Great Britain.

I would like to thank Dr Janet Myles of the

School of Arts and Humanities at De Montford University, Leicester for her helpful comments and for casting a critical eye over the text, Mrs Lucy Ross for typing the manuscript from what was not always legible handwriting, Tom Neville at Ellipsis for his advice and encouragement, and my wife Dorothea who allowed me to rush off to look at buildings, and become a semi-recluse when at home writing.

The White Tower,
Tower of London

The Norman Style

The Anglo-Norman Romanesque style is not only distinctive but seemingly almost impervious to destruction by the normal passage of time. Often only deliberate demolition has rendered a building less than complete. These buildings were built to last and were often extremely substantial with walls of cut-stone blocks filled with rubble over one metre thick. The style can be said to have been evolved in Normandy over the previous one hundred years, with a strong influence from regions as diverse as Lombardy, Burgundy and the Rhineland, and brought to maturity in Great Britain. Examples can be seen from Cornwall in the south-west to Dunfirmline Abbey in Scotland and Kirkwall Cathedral in the Orkney Islands.

While history books celebrate 1066 as the date of the arrival of the Normans, this was in fact the beginning of a permanent occupation. There had been trade and cultural influence before this, and

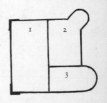

The White Tower:
plan
1 The King's Hall
2 The King's Chamber
3 Chapel

Westminster Abbey founded by Edward the Confessor in 1050 was virtually a Norman building completed in 1065.

Following their arrival by force, the Normans spent the first few decades securing the defensive needs of the country, as well as reforming the Church. This involved the dismissal of the Saxon clergy, including Stigand, Archbishop of Canterbury, and the rebuilding of major cathedrals and monastic foundations. As in many periods of history, piety seemed to go hand-in-hand with a firm military rule. This can be demonstrated no better than by examining their castles.

The most famous are the Tower of London, and Rochester and Dover castles which typically are situated at major strategic points to guard against invasion or civil unrest. Some castles may have been constructed on the sites of earlier wooden fortifications built by Saxons such as that of Pevensey, as depicted on the Bayeaux Tapestry, and were at first rebuilt in wood. By about 1100 the stronghold at the centre of the fortified enclosure known as the keep or donjon was being rebuilt in stone. The White Tower at the heart of the Tower of

Dumfermline Abbey, Fifeshire: columns in the nave, c. 1130–50

London may date from the 1080s, although the stone curtain walls with rectangular and semi-circular mural towers were only built during the thirteenth century. Those at Dover are among the earliest.

Norman keeps were often raised on an artificial hill known as a motte and enclosed by walls to form a bailey or precinct. Beyond the walls would have been a wet moat as for example at the Tower of London, although in many examples, such as Rochester, Dover and Goodrich, there would have been a deep ditch cut into the subsoil or rock which would prove a hurdle to any assailant. Keeps were of three basic types – rectangular, circular shell (as at Windsor), or angular as at Orford, Suffolk. The rectangular type might be up to 30 metres high and would have contained accommodation for the retainer and his family as well as quarters for the garrison. The White Tower still retains its hall and impressive chapel. Contrary to popular belief, a dungeon may simply have been a strong-room or cell in an ancillary building, and not the cellars of a keep which may have been used for storage and may also have contained a well.

Walls were naturally very thick and filled with a rubble core. The White Tower was faced with rough Kentish ragstone and with buttresses, battlements

Durham Cathedral: elevation, plan, sketch view, plan of nave vault bays

and windows dressed with smoothly-cut Caen stone. At the south-east corner the wall bulges into a semi-circular apse to accommodate the eastern termination of the chapel. The base of the Tower and other Norman keeps were splayed to give additional stability as well as extra defence. Keeps which survive in a good condition are to be found at the core of extensive enlargements. With the decline of the castle, they were frequently slighted for building material.

The Norman contribution to church building was immense and to stand in the nave of Durham Cathedral gives one a feeling that it was built to last for all time. It is massive and austere and internally there has been little alteration since completion in about 1135, with the exception of the addition of the eastern Chapel of the Nine Altars in about 1230. The cathedral, which was part of a Benedictine abbey, is cruciform in plan with two western towers and a central tower over the crossing which was subsequently rebuilt. Like many Norman churches, its external walls are divided by strip buttresses and pierced by small semi-circular arched windows. Entry to the nave is through a deeply recessed arched doorway on the north side. The interior is divided into bays by piers with vertical shafts rising from the pavement to the springing of the vault. Each bay is divided into

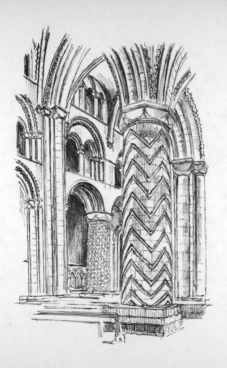

Durham Cathedral:
nave

three stages, common to all Norman greater churches and evolved from Jumièges and the churches of Caen. The lowest is the nave arcade, above is the cruciform, with the clerestory within the curve of the vault. Sometimes, as for example at Ely, these divisions were almost equal in height. At the lowest level, as at Durham, the bay is divided by immense circular drum pillars incised with chevron, spiral and diamond patterns. Similar features can be seen at Dunfermline, Selby and Waltham abbeys.

Unlike other Norman greater churches, Durham was rib-vaulted and we can see the introduction of pointed transverse arches, probably the earliest in Europe, perhaps a decade earlier than St Ambrogio in Milan and Speyer in Germany. Peterborough Cathedral retains its original wooden nave ceiling and this is more typical of a Norman interior. Side aisles were often groin vaulted on a quadripartite plan. Durham also has the earliest example of flying buttressing in Britain, although here they are hidden beneath the side aisle roofs.

Although the style appears austere by later standards, it is renowned for the high quality of decoration and incised carving. Popular decoration includes chevron, beak-head, cable and billet. Capitals were of the unmoulded cushion variety beneath a pro-

OPPOSITE
Canterbury Cathedral, c. 1100: capitals in the crypt. Capital patterns include both plant and animal forms. Also noteworthy is the carving of the shafts which includes spiral and fluted patterns

Barfreston church, Kent

jected abacus, or deeply incised with foliated patterns or strange creatures which were a mixture of bird, animal and monster. Some, as in the crypt at Canterbury Cathedral, play musical instruments. A popular form of wall decoration was blind arcading of either continuous single arches or intersecting arches.

There are hundreds of parish churches with substantial Norman work and some, for example Barfreston in Kent, or Kilpeck, Herefordshire, remain virtually unchanged. These were simple two-cell plans consisting of an aisleless nave and chancel. Barfreston has a square east end: Kilpeck is apsidal. Windows are small. Barfreston has a blind arcade linking the narrow windows. Doorways are recessed and flanked by jamb shafts and surmounted by a carved tympanum. At Barfreston, amid the strange carvings, we find Samson opening a lion's jaw, a bear playing a harp and a monkey with a rabbit. On the centre of the tympa-

Kilpeck church, Herefordshire, with the typical Norman apsidal termination to the chancel

num sits Christ with his hand raised in blessing, as in contemporary Romanesque churches in France. The south door at Kilpeck is surrounded by reddish sandstone carvings of animals, birds and monsters, perhaps suggesting the theme of creation. The door jambs depict Eden with man being tempted by the fruit from the Tree of Life. Both churches also have strange heads carved on to the corbel blocks beneath the eaves of the roof.

Some Norman churches had a small belcot rising from the west gable or a square western tower. Others, particularly when a cruciform plan was introduced, had a tower at the division of nave and chancel. Sometimes, as at Studland, Dorset, it hardly went above the level of the nave roof due to insubstantial foundations. Where side aisles or clerestory appear it is likely that the church once formed part of a monastic complex which may even have been dissolved long before the Reformation.

Few examples of domestic architecture from this period survive, since most houses must have been of timber infilled with wattle and mud, and straw daub. Stone was expensive and used only by rich merchants, particularly the Jewish community. There are records of stone houses in London, Winchester, Canterbury, Norwich, Lincoln and Southampton. Two

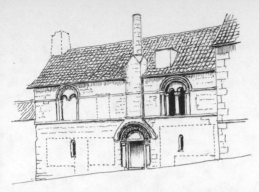

houses from the Jewish community in Lincoln survive on Steep Hill. Their basic construction is similar. The ground floor was used for storage. An arched doorway allowed access to the rear with a staircase to the upper storey which was a communal hall. One, the so-called Jew's House (*c.* 1150), is similar to a surviving twelfth-century house in Cluny, Burgundy, even down to the positioning of a chimney over the ground-floor entrance. Windows were small, twin-arched openings on the upper floor, with slits for the storage space below. Another stone building in Lin-

Lincoln: the Jew's House, c. 1150. Dotted lines represent later alterations, including the insertion of shop fronts

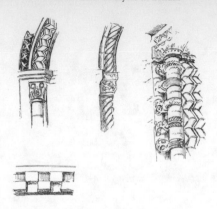

Norman ornament: chevron and dog tooth (Romsey Abbey, Hampshire); cable (Ely, Cambridgeshire); beak head (Lincoln); billet (Canterbury)

coln is the St Mary's Guild House (*c.* 1180). This has a moulded semi-circular central entrance and the façade was strengthened by strip buttresses. The upper hall floor has been largely destroyed, so we see only about half its original elevation. Southampton has the remains of another stone house, known as King John's House, of about 1150, some 16 years before the king was born. Little survives apart from an outstanding fireplace.

24

2

The Transition
to Gothic

It is hard to give a precise date for the adoption of the Gothic style in Britain. The features which make up the style were first seen at Durham Cathedral – pointed arches, ribbed vaults and flying buttressing – yet this building has the weight and solidity of a Romanesque cathedral. The fully developed style employed these elements but reduced them to structure-bearing devices, so that the walls could be pierced by openings of ever-increasing proportion. This process began in France in the quire of the Abbey of St Denis outside Paris in the 1140s and reached maturity in the cathedral of Notre-Dame, Paris, in about 1200.

The transition in Britain was more gradual. The most frequently found feature was the pointed lancet arch; however, ribbed vaulting and flying buttressing

Canterbury Cathedral: east end of Trinity Chapel showing the transition from Romanesque to Early Gothic. In the lower right corner is the fifteenth-century St Edward's Chapel

were first found in the reconstructed quire of Canterbury Cathedral after 1174. The pointed arch has the obvious advantage of directing pressure either side of the centre and to the point of a wall where it can be supported by a buttress. Use of the pointed arch was spread across France by the religious orders, in particular Cistercians. This was also the case in Britain;

Canterbury Cathedral: Trinity Chapel, showing sexpartite rib vaulting completed c. 1190

Fountains Abbey, Yorkshire, under construction in stone for the Cistercian order in the 1150s shows a mixture of pointed and semi-circular arches. However, it was the French cathedrals of Noyon, Laon, Sens and Chartres which really forced the transition.

In September 1174 the quire of Canterbury Cathedral was destroyed by fire. This was interpreted by the monks of Christ Church Priory as a message from God to build a new church worthy of the shrine of Becket. They brought over William of Sens who had supervised the rebuilding of Sens Cathedral in the 1160s. The quire, eastern crypt, Trinity Chapel and Corona were completed by about 1190, and show a lightness of construction which is new. The quire is naturally very French in feeling. The paired columns, the double arches in the triforium and the sexpartite rib vaulting are similar to those in Sens. The apsidal east end is also French in feel. Externally, the windows can be seen to be a mixture of pointed and semi-circular headed arches.

A more definite adoption of the Gothic can be seen in Chichester Cathedral built in the 1190s – arches are pointed and we see deep bands of moulding. Piers and columns are also dressed with detached marble columns anchored by their capitals and bases to the pier or column. At Rochester Cathedral the quire has a fine array of lancet arches, although the elevation is of only two stages with no intermediate triforium. The shafts dividing the bays rise from the pavement to the springing of the vault at about mid-point up the clerestory stage. As at Canterbury, the vault is sexpartite. At Canterbury and Rochester we also see the introduction of another popular repetitive ornament known as the dog tooth which gradually supplanted the chevron of the Norman style.

The cathedral which best exemplifies the change from Norman to an English adaptation of Gothic is Lincoln, rebuilt from about 1095 following an earthquake which damaged the Romanesque building, of which only the west front remains. Here not only do we find lancet windows but also the evolution of plate and bar tracery brought over from France. The vaulting introduces additional ribs creating the effect of an avenue of trees, their branches linked across the centre. Lincoln definitely has that lightness associated with Gothic. Advanced as it is, the cathedral also retains a feature from the French influence on British development – sexpartite vaulting in the western transepts. Lincoln's development was to take it through the Early English period to the dawn of the Decorated style in the fourteenth century.

3

The Gothic Cathedral

Just as thousands of parish churches survive in the Gothic style, so there are numerous cathedrals which remain as witnesses to the highest standards of medieval craftsmanship. Fortunately, most cathedrals were preserved at the Reformation to become seats of the dioceses of the Anglican Church and were not subjected to the destruction inflicted on the monastic churches such as Fountains in Yorkshire and Tynemouth in Northumberland, examples of the early adoption of the Gothic style. The only major medieval cathedral to be destroyed was St Paul's in London, and this by fire in 1666.

The earliest pure Gothic cathedrals were Wells and Salisbury; the latter may be taken as an excellent example of a cathedral built wholly in one style. It was started in 1220 on a new site as the mother church of New Sarum, the town which had just moved from its windswept and cramped site on the edge of Salisbury Plain. The site was new and so

OPPOSITE
Salisbury Cathedral nave, completed c. 1250. At the west end are triple lancet arches, typical of the Early English style

there was no need (as for example at Canterbury and Lincoln) to build over, or on to, existing remains. The plan is cruciform with double transepts and a square eastern termination in a low Lady Chapel rather than an apse with radiating chapels as in its contemporary, Rheims. Most of the stone is local from quarries at Chilmark in south Wiltshire.

As one enters through the north porch one senses that very English characteristic – length as opposed to height. One's eyes are drawn down the relatively low nave to the crossing beneath the tower and spire. The proportions of the elevation have changed: the lower arcade is almost half the height and the triforium has been reduced as the clerestory grows in height to be pierced by triple lancet windows. The horizontality is more than usually emphasised by the lack of shafts between each bay (also the case in the nave of Wells). Both Salisbury and Wells have simple quadripartite rib vaulting in nave and transepts, but the quire of Wells was rebuilt in the fourteenth century with the most advanced lierne pattern. Dramatic scissor arches were inserted to take the weight of the projected crossing tower.

At Salisbury we have an excellent example of the use of clustered shafts of Purbeck marble against the piers. These are divided by annulets and surmounted

*Salisbury
Cathedral: cloister
c. 1263–84; upper stage
of tower and spire
c. 1330–70.
The plan shows the
rectangular eastern
termination and cloister
on the south side. There
is also an eastern
transept similar to that
at Lincoln. The main
entrance is through a
porch on the north side
rather than a grand west
portal as in
contemporary French
cathedrals*

*Wells Cathedral:
crossing strainer arches,
c. 1338*

by roll-moulded capitals. In the Lady Chapel the marble shafts are actually detached from the pier or central column. Externally, the bays are clearly marked by boldly projected buttressing, taking the pressure of the vaulting over the side aisles through a system of flyers. Internally, the weight of the tower is taken by strainer-arches of *c.* 1460 linking the crossing piers against the transepts.

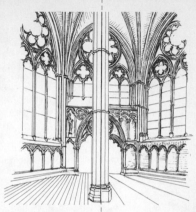

The interior of Salisbury was drastically restored by James Wyatt, *c.* 1790, and Gilbert Scott, *c.* 1860 involving the destruction of chantry chapels, medieval glass, pavements, and the stone pulpitum at the entrance to the quire. This has resulted in a rather severe and over-tidy effect.

While Salisbury was under construction, to be served by a bishop and chapter of secular canons, Westminster Abbey was under reconstruction in the

Chapter houses
LEFT *Westminster Abbey, c. 1253*
RIGHT *Salisbury Cathedral, c. 1263*

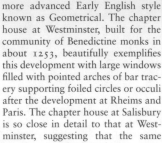

more advanced Early English style known as Geometrical. The chapter house at Westminster, built for the community of Benedictine monks in about 1253, beautifully exemplifies this development with large windows filled with pointed arches of bar tracery supporting foiled circles or occuli after the development at Rheims and Paris. The chapter house at Salisbury is so close in detail to that at Westminster, suggesting that the same craftsmen may have been involved. Both are octagonal with a central column of clustered shafts supporting the ribbed vault. The west front at Salisbury appears rather like a large screen placed across the nave and side aisles. It is without flanking towers as in many English examples but is terminated by low spiralets. The nave bay is filled with triple lancets and not a circular occulus as in French cathedral fronts. Also, little is made of the portals which lack the magnificent carved gables, jambs and tympana of the French cathedrals.

The Early English style can also be seen in many other cathedrals and monastic churches, including York, Ripon and Beverley minsters, Worcester, Peter-

York Minster
TOP *pier with clustered shafts and roll-moulded capitals*
BELOW *ball-flower ornament*

borough, Southwark and Hex-ham Abbey.

By about 1300 Gothic had been fully assimilated and, from an island lagging behind France in development, Britain now took the lead at the time when much of the great cathedral building campaign of the Ile de France was over. The next phase of development is known as 'Decorated' and may be considered to have lasted for much of the fourteenth century. As the name implies, it was a period of rich orna-mentation when much of the carving was highly naturalistic. It was not a period of complete building so much as one of addi-tion or alteration. Only one cathedral, Exeter, may be considered to be largely in the style. Just as Lincoln heralds the early Gothic, so in the so-called Angel Quire at Lincoln of about 1280 we see the transition to the Decorated. The windows have geometrical tracery but the sides exhibit ball-flower ornament. The vault also seems more complex with the introduction of tierceron and ridge ribs. This creates the effect of a

Bristol Cathedral: quire vault, lierne style, with aisle strainer arches beneath, possibly influenced by nearby Wells Cathedral

Exeter Cathedral:
west front, mostly
c. 1350–75. The screen
of niches including
statues of kings is
c. fifteenth century

stone forest of branches which is seen to its greatest effect at Exeter with the longest unbroken area of vaulting in Europe running the length of both nave and quire. At Bristol we see even more complexity with the introduction of lierne ribs to create a star-like pattern.

Window design seems to know no bounds as the tracery twists and curves to form leaf and flame patterns, hence the second term for the period – 'Flamboyant', or curvilinear. Again this is seen at Exeter in the large west front window. At Dorchester Abbey, Oxfordshire, the tracery curves into branches to exhibit the Tree of Jesse in coloured glass. Other fine examples can be seen at York and Canterbury, at the latter cut out of the Norman wall of the St Andrew Chapel. Another form of window tracery of this period was 'reticulated' in which the pattern is like a spreading net, as in the Lady Chapel at Wells.

Carved decoration moved forward from the stiffness of Early Gothic to a highly naturalistic and delicate phase. In Southwell Minster chapter house the leaves seem to all but grow away from the capi-

Southwell Minster, Nottinghamshire
TOP *foliated capitals on chapter house entrance*
BELOW *four-leaf flower ornament*

tals; this delicacy can also be found on wall arcading for example at Ely Cathedral Lady Chapel, and grand tomb canopies such as that of Lady Eleanor Percy in Beverley Minster. At Ely the Lady Chapel still exhibits a wonderful range of decoration in the wall arcading. Each bay is capped by an ogee arch, from the edge of which curving leaves seem to sprout. Unfortunately the figures, including those of the Holy Family, angels and saints, were mutilated by the Puritans, but what remains bears adequate testimony to the virtuosity of the craftsmen. Traces of paint on the decorations survive to give us an idea of this once colourful interior.

Externally buttresses were often more than mere wall supports, displaying life-size figures set into canopied niches. Buttresses frequently terminated in an elaborate pinnacle decorated with crockets and finials. Parapets on walls were also filled with curving tracery, which when seen from the ground gave an added degree of delicacy. Rarely did sculpture play a major part in the external treatment of English medieval cathedrals, although the west front of Wells had several hundred figures set into canopied niches, a number of which have been restored. At Exeter the west front has a band of figures representing ancient beings. These look rather awkward and certainly do

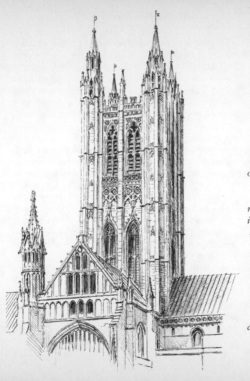

Canterbury Cathedral: crossing tower (Bell Harry), c. 1490–1508, originally conceived as a single-stage lantern tower c. 1470. The raising of a second stage involved the insertion of strainer arches beneath the crossing. John Wastell, master-mason, who was at that time supervising the completion of King's College Chapel, Cambridge, was certainly the architect of the upper stage

not compare with those adorning the great west fronts of French cathedrals.

The last phase of Gothic, the Perpendicular, lasted the longest and includes the Tudor phase, which overlaps with the dawn of the Renaissance. When the style began is open to scholarly debate. In general it may be seen as the prevalent style of the fifteenth century, and for a long time the Black Death of 1349–50 was seen as the cause of the end of the Decorated style. This is not so. The earliest surviving examples of Perpendicular Gothic characteristics are the gateway of St Augustine's Abbey, Canterbury (*c.* 1306) and Gloucester Cathedral quire, rebuilt from about 1337. St Stephen's Chapel in the Palace of Westminster, built from *c.* 1306 and destroyed by fire in 1834, and the chapter house of Old St Paul's Cathedral, *c.* 1332, both under the direction of the master-mason William de Ramsay, were virtually the first complete buildings in the style. At its simplest this phase may be seen as consisting of walls and windows divided by vertical mullions and horizontal transoms, hence its secondary title, rectilinear. If it was not quite as inventive as the Decorated, it was certainly more prolific.

As in the Decorated period there was little complete rebuilding of greater churches, with the excep-

*Gloucester Cathedral:
cloister with fan
vaulting over lavatorium
(monks' washing place)*

King's College Chapel, Cambridge: started in 1446, work was interrupted by the royal vicissitudes of the fifteenth century. It was finally completed c. 1515 under the patronage of Henry VIII. The interior remains complete with its original Flemish glass

tion of Sherborne and Bath Abbeys. It was more a period for rebuilding of major areas of cathedrals such as naves, as at Canterbury and Winchester; the latter involved the encasing of the Norman piers in a Perpendicular outer skin. At Norwich the Norman clerestory was replaced; at Oxford Cathedral, then St Frideswides Priory, a fan and pendant vault was built over the Norman quire; Peterborough received a fan-vaulted Lady Chapel. Numerous crossing towers were built including Canterbury, Gloucester, York, Durham, Lincoln (western), Malvern Priory and Fountains Abbey's north transeptal tower. As well as St Stephen's, Westminster, several other royal chapels were built in the style including St George, Windsor, and Henry VII at the east end of Westminster Abbey.

Perhaps the building which most typifies the style, however, is King's College Chapel, Cambridge (1446–1515). Here we find repeating bays of mullions climbing from the pavement across the blind wall surface to link with the window mullions and so forming continuous vertical divisions between the floor and the curve of the arches. These are inter-sected at intervals by horizontal transoms. Each bay has a division of clustered shafts in the ante chapel rising to the transverse division of the fan vaulting of the ceiling. In the quire the vaulting shafts spring

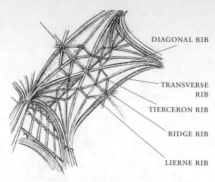

DIAGONAL RIB

TRANSVERSE
RIB

TIERCERON RIB

RIDGE RIB

LIERNE RIB

*Canterbury Cathedral:
nave bay and vault. The
nave replaces that of
Lanfranc's building of
c. 1070–77*

from corbel stops on a level with the window transoms. The size of the windows filling each bay creates
the impression of a giant stone-framed greenhouse.
The fan vaulting which is used here to such superb
effect was developed from that in Gloucester Cathedral cloister of about 1460, although it has been suggested that a lierne vault was originally intended, and
that John Wastell, master mason at King's College,
was influenced by the fan-vaulted quire of Sherborne
Abbey of about 1460.

Few can remain unmoved by the clean and sim-

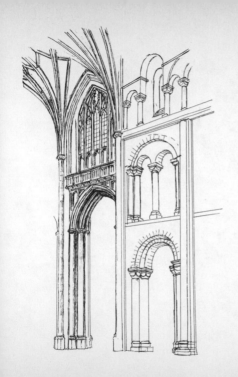

*Winchester Cathedral:
nave. Gothic bay
construction,
c. 1394–1450 (left)
encasing partially
demolished Norman
bay, c. 1100 (right)*

*Oxford Cathedral:
quire. Norman,
c. 1150–80, with fan
and pendant vaulting
added c. 1480–1500*

ple lines of the naves of Canterbury and Winchester Cathedrals. By now much light comes in through tall side aisle windows. The triforium is reduced to little more than an intermediate gallery. In both these examples the clerestory windows are relatively small; however, at Sherborne and Bath Abbeys they are almost half the total elevation. At Gloucester and York Cathedrals about three-quarters of the east end of the quires are filled by enormous rectilinear traceried windows.

On the exteriors, parapets and towers invited a further display of rectilinear panelling; at Canterbury, Bell Harry tower has decorative motifs of Tudor roses and a cardinal's hat set into the surface between vertical mullions and ogee hoods recalling the royal house and the patron of the tower-building campaign, Cardinal Moreton.

In general, decoration and moulding is shallower than in earlier periods and rather predictable and repetitive. It could, however, rise to a highly complex and delicate form, as in the fan and pendant vault of Oxford Cathedral, and Henry VII's Chapel, Westminster. By the time this royal chapel was nearing completion in 1520, the first Italian Renaissance ornament was appearing in England, on the tomb of Henry VII beneath that remarkable vault.

Uffington, Berkshire:
Early English church
with lancet windows
and octagonal crossing
tower. Entrance is
through the south porch
(left). The now-familiar
rectangular chancel end
is seen to the right

4

The Medieval Parish Church

Thousands of churches survive with a substantial structure dating back to before the Reformation. No two are the same although there are regional features in planning and ornament. For instance, the flint and stone churches in the Perpendicular style of Norfolk differ from the small moorland churches of north Yorkshire. Spires abound in Northamptonshire and Lincolnshire but are rare in Somerset and Devon. Churches also reflect the wealth of a region as well as local patronage. It is no coincidence that the largest parish churches are in Hull, Great Yarmouth and Boston, once flourishing ports trading with the Hanseatic ports of Flanders and the Baltic. Local patronage, whether it be from a nobleman, merchant or trade guild, often led to the rebuilding of a chancel or nave, or the construction of a chantry or burial

St Botolph,
Boston, Lincolnshire

chapels which in some cases, as in the Cotswolds, almost doubled the area of the church.

As we have seen, Norman churches were usually relatively simple in plan with a rectangular nave and chancel terminating in an apse. If the church was cruciform a tower would mark the crossing. Although side aisles and clerestorys were rare in parish churches of this period, they do occur, for example at Melbourne, Derbyshire. Here, thick drum pillars support the arcading. The carved decoration is of the highest quality.

With the coming of the Early English period chancels were often rebuilt to provide more space and light. Windows were at first lancets but by the mid-thirteenth century increasingly displayed plate and then geometrical bar tracery. If naves had side aisles the piers might display detached shafts. Dog-tooth moulding was increasingly prevalent. Towers at the west end might now support an octagonal spire, splayed on four sides with broaches to link with the corners of the tower.

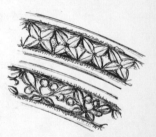

TOP *St Mary, Stamford, Lincolnshire: octagonal broach spire*
BELOW *Dog-tooth moulding, two versions*

53

*St Patrick, Patrington,
East Yorkshire,
c. 1320–1410. The
chancel is lit by a large
rectilinear window of
the later Perpendicular
period*

As with cathedrals, the Decorated period was
not one of totally new building but rather of embell-
ishment. Perhaps the two most notable, almost
wholly 'Decorated' churches are those at Hecking-
ton, Lincolnshire and Patrington, Yorkshire. Both

have tall towers with spires rising from behind a
parapet and flanked at each corner by tall pinnacles.
The corners of the spire display sprouting crockets
like leaves and the surfaces are pierced at intervals by
lucarnes – gabled openings which allow air to circu-
late inside the spire.

Walls were pierced by large geometrical and
flamboyant windows filling the full wall space
between buttresses. Grantham, Lincolnshire, is an

*St Wulfram, Grantham,
Lincolnshire: windows
on the south side of the
Lady Chapel, c. 1350*

St John the Baptist,
Cirencester,
Gloucestershire:
although the original
church was erected
c. 1180, it was largely
rebuilt in the fifteenth
century. Great south
porch c. 1500

excellent example. A characteristic feature of this period is ball flower ornament, as seen at Badgeworth, Gloucestershire and Ledbury, Herefordshire.

The Perpendicular Gothic phase is more than adequately represented in parish churches, more so as the second half of the fifteenth century was a period of great rebuilding and enlargement. Some of the so-called 'wool churches' of the Cotswolds – such as Cirencester, Burford and Northleach – attain considerable size and lightness with large aisle windows and the introduction of a clerestory. In eastern England, particularly in Norfolk and Suffolk, churches were built in a combination of stone and flint with the lines of window tracery sometimes continued across walls with stone strips inserted into a flint ground, a treatment known as flushwork. In rare instances brick might now be used for additions; Holy Trinity, Hull is unique in having been rebuilt largely in brick.

Windows have increasingly slight curves to a central point and are sometimes rectangular with a rectilinear tracery pattern within. Roof pitch is radically reduced, sometimes to less than ten degrees, thus allowing the tracery of an open parapet to be silhouetted against the sky. Battlementing was a favourite form.

St Mary, Burford, Oxfordshire: a fine example of a parish church with a Norman core visible in the crossing tower and later additions including chantry chapels

The entrances to churches were now often through majestic south or north porches. These would be flanked by buttresses and, if part of a major town church, might have an upper storey for use as a grammar school room or place for parish meetings. The money given for the provision of a school might be part of the endowment for a guild or chantry chapel in which masses would be celebrated for the repose of the souls of the benefactors. Excellent examples of such chapels, which are almost like stone cages in their lightness, are to be found at Burford in Oxfordshire, Cirencester in Gloucestershire and Lavenham in Suffolk.

Most parish churches were covered by a timbered roof and stone vaulting was used sparingly, if at all, for memorial chapels or side aisles. Only one English medieval church, St Mary Redcliffe, Bristol, is vaulted throughout. Roof types ranged from the

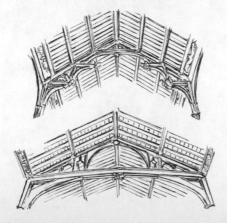

Roof types
ABOVE *hammer beam*
BELOW *tie beam*

simple tie beam to the complex hammer beam in the richest examples.

Seen from afar across open country some churches of this period take on the appearance of cathedrals in miniature as they dwarf the surrounding cottages of a village, or the roofscape of a small town. As with cathedrals, towers became objects of pride, even rivalry. Those in the Cotswolds and Somerset are outstanding for height and delicacy. Some are crowned with open-battlemented parapets and corner pinnacles of tracery similar to that of the crossing tower of Gloucester Cathedral. Notable are St Stephen's, Bristol, St Mary's, Taunton, and Malvern Priory. One of the tallest towers is that of St Botolph, Boston (Lincolnshire), surmounted by an octagonal lantern stage which is copied on a smaller scale at St Mary and All Saints, Fotheringay (Northamptonshire), and All Saints Pavement, York. Boston's huge tower must have been inspired by those in Flanders and the Low Countries such as that of the Cloth Hall in Bruges and church towers at Malines or Utrecht.

Today it is hard to glimpse the original colour and atmosphere of a pre-Reformation church. Originally the walls would have been painted with biblical themes and the chancel arch adorned with a large

St Thomas of Canterbury, Salisbury: this magnificent interior displays to the full the power of a Doom painting above the chancel arch

Judgement painting. The best surviving example is St Thomas of Canterbury in Salisbury. Beneath the chancel arch would have been a rood screen displaying exquisite carving and painted panels. A few survive, for example in Dunster, Somerset, and Plymtree, Devon. The top of the screen would have had an overhanging platform or loft beneath which would have been carved vaulting. Above the loft would have been a large crucifix and statues of the Blessed Virgin and St John.

Much medieval glass was destroyed by the Puritans and where it does survive it is often in a new position, or simply a jumble of coloured glass. There are however exceptions; perhaps one of the finest examples of a complete series of medieval windows is that of Fairford, Gloucestershire.

Tombs reflect local patronage and wealth and might take the form of recumbent effigies of the deceased. For the nobility, coats of arms might also be displayed in a richly decorated canopy or on the tomb chest itself. In the fifteenth century merchants were increasingly represented dressed in fur-edged gowns with feet resting on a lamb.

Fortunately churches did not suffer the destructive fate of monasteries, although an Act of 1549 allowing the destruction of chantries and rood

St John, Plymtree, Devon: surviving rood screen, one of a number of impressive examples of medieval craftsmanship in the county

screens was a grievous blow to the skills of the medieval sculptor, wood carver and painter. There was however to be a period of neglect, particularly in the eighteenth century, leading to restoration and rebuilding in the nineteenth century.

Several Oxford and Cambridge colleges retain their original chapels which formed a major aspect of their layout. That of Merton College, Oxford may be taken as typical. Founded in 1274, the original Mob Quadrangle was completed by about 1300. Work on the chapel in the Perpendicular style continued throughout the fourteenth century, and its T-shaped plan was adopted at nearby New College and Magdalen. By far the largest and grandest of college chapels was that of King's, Cambridge (c. 1446–1515).

Merton College, Oxford,
with chapel

Dover Castle, Kent: its system of double curtain walls makes it virtually impregnable

5

The Castle and
Medieval Manor House

The Normans laid the firm foundation of national defence with their keeps set on a mound or motte. At first these were surrounded by wooden walls but in time stone came to replace what must have seemed a weak point of defence. Dover remains an excellent example of a well-developed system of stone curtain walls flanked at intervals by mural towers, at first rectangular in plan but subsequently polygonal or semi-circular to reduce the chance of collapse as a result of tunnellers beneath. One of the corner towers of Rochester keep collapsed as a result of mining during the siege of 1215 and was rebuilt in semi-circular form.

By the late thirteenth century there was an increasing wish for more room within a castle complex of inner and outer bailey, the keep often proving cramped. This led to the building of a detached hall and chapel within the inner compound known as the bailey. Windows were now much larger than those built by the Normans and would follow the bar-tracery geometrical-patterned fashion of churches – after all, the outer walls would act as a form of defence. Some halls, such as those at Oakham and Winchester, were aisled and could accommodate many guests at high table and in the body of the hall. By parish church standards, castle chapels were small and usually rectangular, although that at Ludlow Castle, Shropshire, is circular in plan. In some instances the chapel, for example at Durham, had a high degree of carved ornament, especially on the entrance portal; however, usually they are small and austere.

Entry to a castle was through a gatehouse, an obvious area of weakness in the curtain walls, which therefore had to be very strong. Often gatehouses were flanked by tall drum towers, splayed at the base and crenellated at the top. These contained spiral-staircase access to each floor, the treads supported in the thickness of the wall. Above the entrance the parapet might have been machicolated or projected so the platform could be pierced with 'murder holes' from which stones or boiling fat could be dropped on assailants. The entrance itself could be barred by a portcullis of wood studded with iron. It is romantic to think of all castles as having been surrounded by a wet moat; conditions might not have allowed this and a ditch would have sufficed to stop an assailant placing a ladder or belfry near the walls.

If the castle was the residence of a powerful lord who may have had to entertain the king, more room would have been needed than the keep could provide. By the end of the thirteenth century therefore, the inner bailey may, as we have seen, have contained a hall, chapel and other ancillary buildings specifically for the lord's use. A certain duplication of buildings such as a hall, and a chapel for the garrison, might be built in the outer bailey. By then the defence of the bailey had improved, with thick curtain walls rising well above these buildings.

The greatest castle-building campaign in Britain was that of Edward I between about 1280 and 1300 to guard the coastline of Wales and the Welsh marches or English border counties. These introduced a new form of plan in which the keep was dispensed with (except at Flint), in place of enlarged domestic apartments within very high curtain walls, as for example at Caernarvon, Beaumaris and Conway. The walled enclosure was further divided by a wall or list into an upper and lower ward. At

Caernarvon, said to have been modelled on the walls of Constantinople, the mural towers are polygonal and some are surmounted by turrets for increased observation. Those at Conway are circular drums.

Caernarvon Castle

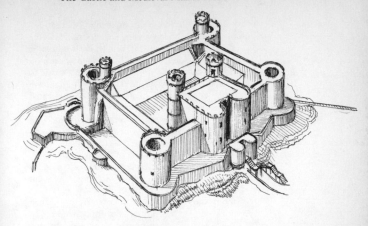

At Harlech and Beaumaris (*c.* 1280–90) we see examples of the concentric plan with a double rim of walls and the defensive stronghold in the gatehouse with residential apartments. The outer gate was not aligned with the inner gatehouse, lessening the chance of an assailant mounting a charge. At Beaumaris the southern gatehouse was approached at an angle to avoid a concentrated attack and to avoid

Harlech Castle: the inner gateway has virtually taken over the defensive purpose of the keep

being fully exposed to fire from above. To get to the outer gate necessitated crossing a drawbridge.

With the increase in wall height, castles became virtually impervious to assault by trebuchet, catapult or battering ram. The only way to reduce a castle to submission seemed to be by starving the garrison through a lengthy siege. To allow more concentrated fire power, embrasures or arrow loops were increased in number from single openings through the merlons of the battlements to lines of openings for firing galleries behind the walls. These were splayed on the inside to allow for the angling of the crossbow.

Such was the confidence now in castle defence that a second lesser entrance or postern gate was cut through the curtain wall. This might allow a garrison the opportunity to launch a counter-attack against the assailant who was prevented from concentrating his attack at any one point due to his need to surround the whole perimeter closely.

Although the great age of castle building could be said to have ended with the death of Edward I in 1307, many castles still underwent extensive rebuilding or addition. An excellent example is the Tower of London where the seemingly massive Norman White Tower became immersed within a complex series of concentric walls guarded every few yards by cylindrical or polygonal mural towers. Surrounded by a broad moat, it was reached through an outer barbican and then across the moat by a stone causeway and drawbridge.

The medieval castle had become so impregnable that it largely outlived its purpose. In any case the nature of warfare was increasingly becoming a struggle to be decided by open battle in the field, or even across the Channel in France. There were still a few new castles built in the fourteenth century, especially in the Scottish border country, such as Etal (*c.* 1340), a keep and bailey type. Nearby Edlington (*c.* 1350) also has an outdated keep. Another familiar defensive feature of this region is the so-called stone Pele Tower, which was little more than a rectangular tower of perhaps three or more storeys combining room for storage and a residence. Although for the most part built to guard against cattle and crop thieves, the most impressive towers, such as Belsay, have corner turrets, machicolation and crenellation.

At the other end of the country in Sussex there was the threat of French nuisance raids during the Hundred Years War. Bodiam, one of the most picturesque (and photographed) castles, was built as a result, between about 1385 and 1400. It is set in a broad lake fed by the River Rother and reached

Bodiam Castle, East Sussex: the wide moat provides perfect defence

across a right-angled causeway, through a barbican, and across a double drawbridge. Its plan is quadrangular, each corner marked by a huge drum tower and a gatehouse flanked by machicolated towers. From outside it appears to be impregnable, the chapel window seeming to provide the only hint of the domesticity within. Inside the walls most is now in ruin but it had a continuous range of apartments round the four walls including a great hall, kitchen, buttery and chapel so as to provide an inner rectangular space. Chambers survive over the gatehouse, giving some indication of the size and structure of the apartments which were lit by narrow windows and heated from a simple fireplace. Gardrobes which discharged directly into the moat also survive.

By the time Bodiam was finished the fortified manor house (the French *manoir* means a dwelling) had been introduced, allowing for a far greater degree of comfort while at the same time providing limited protection from unrest. But, most importantly, a grant by the king of a 'licence to crenellate' and thus build and live in a fortified house, gave immense political and social status. An excellent example is the case of Sir John Poultney, a merchant of London and financial supporter of the wars of Edward III, who was granted the manor of Penshurst in Kent and a licence in 1341. The dominant surviving feature is the Great Hall, entered through a porch. The floor is of hard brick but the central hearth is of stone for a fire, the smoke of which rose to a louvred exit in the ridge of the roof. At the entrance or lower end of the hall was a vestibule divided by a screen from the body of the hall. The outer wall was pierced by doors to the now-destroyed kitchen. The screen in effect provided a barrier against the smell from the kitchen. Behind the upper end of the hall, where a high table raised on steps was placed, was a parlour with a solar and other domestic apartments above. In some cases, as at Penshurst, there may have been a cellar beneath.

The solar, from the old French *soler*, an upstairs room lit by the sun, was the private living and sleeping chamber of the household. By the end of the Middle Ages the solar may have been just one of a number of domestic chambers which would also have included a chapel and chamber for the chaplain. The solar would usually have a spy-hole, as at Penshurst, to allow the family to watch the hall below.

Glass was rare as a permanent filling to windows even in royal residences. Royal accounts record frequent payment for the insertion and removal of glass panels as the kings moved from one palace or manor to another. Windows were therefore closed by shutters, as can still be seen in Hemingford Manor, Cambridge, or by lattice panels composed of diagonal strips of wood, as at Stokesay Castle, Shropshire. In order to combat the fierce winter cold, an additional fireplace might be built into the side wall.

Penshurst Place, Kent:
Great Hall

Most manors would be entered across a ditch, or broad moat as at Ightham, Kent, and through a gatehouse as at Stokesay (later rebuilt), or of considerable grandeur, as in the brick gatehouse at Oxburgh Hall, Norfolk (1482). The courtyard beyond would have contained stables and a well. The hall may have been in a tall L-shaped tower block as in Little Wenham, Suffolk, one of the earliest buildings in brick. The chapel with solar above is at right angles to the hall.

Another impressive brick-built manor is Tattershall Castle, Lincolnshire (c. 1450), built for Ralph Cromwell, Treasurer to Henry VI. It is very tall, rectangular in plan, with polygonal corner turrets and what can only be described as exaggerated machicolations beneath the parapet. The castle was originally part of a large complex including a chantry chapel and almshouses for poor men.

By the close of the period some, for instance Haddon Hall in Derbyshire, had a hall dividing the enclosure into an upper and lower court, with ranges of chambers on all sides. This was similar to Eltham (now south-east London) where the royal manor had a great hall (c. 1480) dividing courts, but also a substantial chapel (c. 1500) built out into the great court.

Like parish churches, manor houses exhibit fine

Stokesay Castle, Shropshire: window

78

Ightham Mote, Kent

Oxburgh Hall, Norfolk

HALL

CHAPEL

*Little Wenham Hall,
Suffolk*

Tattershall Castle,
Lincolnshire

craftsmanship in the variety of timber roofs spanning halls and the carving of screens and panelling. Also like churches they have been subject to change and alteration, which in some cases was even more drastic. In some, floors were inserted, particularly in halls to make more room, or the medieval hall might have been demolished to make way for a Georgian dining room and private suite.

Haddon Hall,
Derbyshire

The Shambles, York:
15th century and later

6

The Medieval House

For obvious reasons a house in continuous use is likely to be subject to frequent alteration. If situated in a town its existence might be threatened by pressure to maximise the use of the site, leading to rebuilding perhaps several times in a century. In medieval times, additional threats of destruction came from fire, siege or flooding. Before the fifteenth century few houses were constructed in stone, except those originally built by the Jewish community, for example in Lincoln. After a fire in 1189 Richard 1 issued building regulations to the citizens of London requiring the building of stone party walls of at least three feet in thickness. However, it was not until the Great Fire of 1666 that rules against building in wood were fully enforced.

Where medieval timber town houses survive unaltered in any number, as in Canterbury, Shrewsbury and York, they are of the fifteenth century, and are on deep rectangular plots with a narrow frontage

to the street. They were built up to two or more storeys jettied or projected at each stage, the top being within the gable of the roof. Where possible a foundation of stone or brick was used to avoid damp causing sill beams to warp prematurely. The ground floor of a town house might serve as a shop with a timber panel opening out to the street to display wares for sale. A door might lead directly into the front chamber or a passage through to a yard behind which might have been used to keep animals or fowl.

Paycocke's House, Coggeshall, Essex: c. 1450

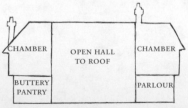

| CHAMBER | OPEN HALL TO ROOF | CHAMBER |
| BUTTERY PANTRY | | PARLOUR |

Wealden Hall house, Kent/Sussex: numerous examples of this type of late-medieval house survive in the wooded regions of the Weald

Little Moreton Hall, Cheshire: c. 1520–1590. Although not strictly medieval, it represents the peak of half-timber construction in north-west England

The upper stages were jettied on immensely thick joists which ran through the house and acted as a support for the floorboards of each chamber. Heavy furniture was placed against the outer walls or at points where the joists were supported by a wall or frame below. Windows might also project, the sill supported by brackets. The party wall of stone or brick would have a fireplace on each floor and a flue to the chimney stack above the level of the roof ridge. Thatch was widespread as a roof covering until at least the thirteenth century when the use of tile became more widespread, especially in towns.

There were variations in planning and where a town or village was not confined by walls or a ditch, houses were sometimes oriented lengthways to the street as, for example, in Lavenham and Coggeshall, East Anglia. The term 'half-timbered' is very apt as there were numerous vertical studs, horizontal transoms and diagonal struts placed within the area of the structural timbers. The timbers were held together by wooden nails or pegs, or by mortise and tenon joints. There are many regional variations. In some the timbers were filled with rectangular panels intersected by a diagonal strut or windbrace, or vertical studs placed a few inches apart: hence the term close studding.

Canterbury, Kent: herringbone brick in-filling to jettied stage of half-timbered house

The most common form of infilling was wattle and daub in which vertical oak staves were woven horizontally by hazel wattles. This was daubed with a mixture of clay, dung and chopped straw, and the panel was then limewashed or painted. Regional variations included a filling of stone chippings plastered over, or, increasingly from the later Middle Ages, herringbone brickwork. In the wooded areas of Kent, Cheshire and Shropshire the timber patterns could be extremely complex with quatrefoil patterns set off against white-painted plaster.

In the country, houses ranged from the simplest timber-framed cruck cottage as seen at Didbrook, Gloucestershire (*c.* 1500) to the yeoman's hall house of the Kent and Sussex Weald. The hall house was originally open in the middle from the ground floor to the roof. At the upper end was a parlour with a jettied chamber above and, at the opposite end, kitchen, pantry and larder with a chamber above. As this type of house was refined, so a stone or brick chimney might be introduced through the end walls or at the side. Solid brick was increasingly used for the lower stages of the side chambers towards the end of the period.

In the wool areas of the Cotswolds and the south-west merchant houses were built of stone. At Chipping Camden, Gloucestershire, Grevil's House of about 1490 had an open hall with a tall bay window filled with Perpendicular mullions. As the period closed so brick was increasingly widespread and windows filled with glass increased in size. At Ockwells Manor, Berkshire, the hall is filled on both sides with an almost continuous row of windows like a gallery.

When seeking examples of medieval architecture it must be remembered that what is a substantial building of this period might well be buried behind a brick or even a stone frontage of the last hundred years or so.

Hardwick Hall,
Derbyshire

7

Tudor Architecture

While the period 1485–1603 was one of dramatic religious and political change, in architecture the transition from the Gothic to the classical style was much slower, and the appearance of most towns outside London would have shown little evidence of the Renaissance. Because of its geographical isolation, Britain followed western Europe in her absorption and true understanding of the principles of classical ornament and proportion. The religious troubles of the Reformation and subsequent suspicion about the Roman Catholic continent discouraged much contact with the classical south. It was in the fields of literature and the theatre that the classical world had the greatest impact on the general public. Both Marlowe and Shakespeare wrote plays based on classical history and mythology. There was no national school of painting and most artists at this time were Flemish or German by birth, and their subject matter largely confined to portraiture.

Renaissance architectural form was developed in Florence from the 1420s by Brunelleschi and was the subject of a number of learned treatises, from Alberti in the 1450s to Serlio and Palladio over one hundred years later. As in France, it was the court which was responsible for the early use of classical form. Henry VIII imported craftsmen from Italy and France to work on his numerous hunting palaces and manors, including Nonsuch in Surrey (demolished *c.* 1685). The earliest surviving actual use of classical ornament is on the tomb of Henry VII in Westminster Abbey designed by the Florentine sculptor Pietro Torigiano (*c.* 1512). Torigiano had actually been a fellow student of Michelangelo in the school run by the Medicis.

It was more as ornamentation that the classical style began to appear, as for example in a classical capital in Chelsea Church, London or the wooden pulpitum screen in King's College Chapel, Cambridge (*c.* 1535). This has a strong flavour of the Lombardic Renaissance from the hands of Italian craftsmen. The Loire châteaux building programme of François 1 contributed a number of craftsmen who worked at Hampton Court, St James's Palace and Nonsuch.

The sixteenth century was no exception in showing royal favour to those who had supported the monarch in times of difficulty, particularly during the struggle with the Church. Size emphasised status rather than convenience. After the Dissolution of the Monasteries, building material, especially stone, was used for stately homes such as Fountains Hall, Yorkshire and Longleat, Wiltshire.

As the century progressed the traditional quadrangular plan as seen at Ightham and Haddon was gradually superseded by the open E plan. This created the need for an imposing front with the entrance set into a central projected bay, against which the classical orders were displayed in ascending stages with the Doric on the lowest. The proportion and accuracy varied according to the source, usually a pattern book published in France or Flanders. Serlio's treatise on architecture was not translated into English until 1610.

As stone was a costly material, unless plundered, many sixteenth-century houses used brick extensively, often of a reddish hue and inset with a chequer pattern of black or white bricks. Terracotta was sometimes used instead of stone as in the centrepiece of Sutton Place, Surrey (c. 1529). Increasingly there was an emphasis on symmetry, with flanking wings at each side. Windows were large and rectangular

*Hampton Court,
Greater London: brick
chimneys*

with lead glazing bars set between mullions and transoms. A horizontal band of brick coursing might be used to define the level of the floors from the exterior. Roofs were still often steeply pitched but now projected out over eaves instead of falling behind battlemented parapets. As roof spaces were utilised for additional servants' quarters, light was admitted through gables projecting at intervals from the main roof line. Other memorable features of the roof line of Tudor houses are the batteries of tall cylindrical brick chimneys exhibiting intricate pattern work. Excellent examples include Hampton Court, Charlecote Park, Warwickshire, and Sawston Hall, Cambridge.

The reign of Elizabeth I witnessed the building of a number of 'prodigy' houses, remarkable for their size as well as a more serious approach to classical form. Most notable were those attributed to Robert Smythson who was described on his tombstone as 'Architect and Surveyor unto the most worthy house of Wollaton and diverse others of great account'. In addition to Wollaton, these include Longleat, Hardwick Worksop (demolished), Burton Agnes, and perhaps Fountains Hall.

HALL

Wollaton Hall,
Nottinghamshire:
Flemish strapwork
pattern in tower gables

Longleat, Wiltshire, was begun in 1541 and although not completed until 1580, is memorable both for its symmetry and enormous windows, 'more window than wall'. It has classically-ordered pilasters applied correctly to the three stages between each window. Each floor is defined by a cornice and the main entrance is via a Doric pedimented door-case. The roof is flat and hidden by an open parapet adorned with triumphal-arch motifs and lions. The chimneys are in the form of Tuscan columns surmounted by an entablature and cornice. As the roof now served as a promenade for the household and guests, domed pavilions known as banqueting houses were introduced from which wine and sweetmeats could be served.

By now the great hall had in many cases become one of many large apartments, or even just an entrance chamber used only on special occasions. As such it cannot always be identified from outside unless it still uses the full height of the house as at Burghley near Stamford. Here the mansion is attributed to its founder William Cecil, Lord Burghley, who took a keen interest in architectural progress although he had the advice of an Antwerp mason named Henryk. It was begun in 1553, and the great hall retains medieval proportions with a steep

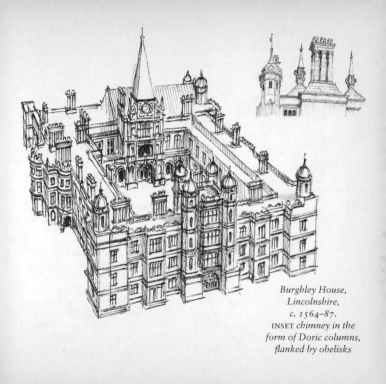

*Burghley House,
Lincolnshire,
c. 1564–87.*
INSET *chimney in the
form of Doric columns,
flanked by obelisks*

Cobham Hall, Kent

pitched roof supported by the now almost outdated hammer-beam construction. Like Longleat, it retains a courtyard plan with the inner ground stage originally arcaded like an Italian palazzo. Also like Longleat, this roof line is punctuated by columned chimneys, obelisks and turrets. However, most memorable is the tall courtyard entrance to the hall rising in ordered stages, perhaps inspired by Philbert Delormé's centrepiece for the château of Anet, *c.* 1550 (this centrepiece is now preserved in the courtyard of the Ecole des Beaux Arts, Paris). It is surmounted by a clock with a single hour hand and the date of completion, 1587. Above this rises an enormous obelisk.

Hardwick Hall, also by Smythson, is notable not only for its enormous windows but also for the earliest use of the long gallery which took over from the hall as the social centre. Not only could household and guests talk and walk here, but portraits could be displayed. Family pedigree was very important to the Elizabethan gentry and not least the owner, Elizabeth of Hardwick, who even had the parapet of the six towers adorned with her cypher, ES.

A fine example of the English adaption of the triple-staged porch adopted from France is that of Cobham Hall, Kent. Dated 1594, it led into the hall. The third stage lacks an order and paired piers support urns. A final classical touch is added by the pediment surmounting this stage.

Away from the mansion several academic buildings in Oxford and Cambridge began to show signs of the classical style towards the close of the century. At Cambridge these include the Gate of Honour at Gonville and Caius College – perhaps by Dr Caius, physician to Edward VI and Queen Mary. He had studied medicine in Padua, and so would have been exposed to the latest classical developments in northern Italy. In the Great Court of Trinity College there is a fountain beneath a canopied octagonal arcade supported on Ionic columns from about 1601. It also exhibits Flemish strapwork on each side and the canopy is surmounted by a rampant lion clasping a shield displaying the Tudor arms. The first college in either university wholly in the classical style was Clare, Cambridge, rebuilt c. 1640–80. At Oxford the Tower of the Five Orders (c. 1600) which forms the entrance to the Bodleian quadrangle was the first example in Britain to exhibit the Composite and Roman Doric orders influenced by Serlio.

Trinity College, Cambridge: Great Court, c. 1600. Fountain beneath Ionic arcade with strapwork-decorated parapet

Charlton House,
Greenwich

8

The Jacobean House

To a certain extent the period between 1603 and 1620 was a continuation of the Tudor age, at least architecturally, and witnessed the building of another batch of prodigy houses. These include Hatfield, Audley End, Charlton, Bramshill and Holland House. They suggest a more settled period of design, a sense of mass and silhouette and less of a show of great windows. As in the later years of Elizabeth's reign, large numbers of continental craftsmen were at work in Britain, including the Scottish court of James VI. There were of course additional sources from pattern books which had detail from the Netherlands, or exotic distortion or reinvention of classical forms from the Nuremberg craftsman Wendel Dietterlin. The most widely used ornamentation was strapwork from the Flemish *Architectura* of Vredeman de Vries. We see this on the centrepiece of Charlton House, south London.

The standard plan for the large house was either

the so-called H plan or the E plan. The H plan was perhaps first used at Wimbledon House, which had deeply projecting side wings, and a few years later at Condover Hall, Shropshire. The square or rectangular plan, as seen at Chastleton near Oxford and Bolsover Castle in Derbyshire, was also popular. Blickling Hall in Norfolk has an unusually elongated rectangular plan.

Although Audley End near Cambridge, built for the Earl of Suffolk, was started a few years earlier in 1603, Hatfield may be taken to exemplify the character of the period. In 1607 work started on a new house to replace the old palace which had for a time been the childhood home of Elizabeth I. Robert Cecil, Earl of Salisbury, had exchanged the manor of Theobalds with James I for the royal manor of Hatfield and like his father, William Cecil, Lord Burghley, set about building a mansion worthy to entertain the king and queen. It is an E plan with separate apartments in each wing for the royal guests, the king in the east wing and the queen in the west. It has a central linking block built of stone, some of which was pillaged from St Augustine's Abbey, Canterbury. The ground floor had an open Italianate loggia (subsequently enclosed) divided by Doric pilasters. On the upper floor the bays are divided by Ionic

Hatfield House, Hertfordshire: the grand staircase

pilasters. The centrepiece with the completion date, 1611, rises three floors to include paired triple orders after the French manner, also seen at Burghley. The roof line behind is broken by Dutch gables, another feature from the Netherlands, and a central clock and belfry tower in receding stages. The projecting wings are of red brick and are three rooms wide on the front between the staircase turrets capped in lead. These are a familiar feature of the Jacobean style and may have originated at Theobalds, built by William Cecil from the 1560s.

Just who created Hatfield is slightly confusing, as with many great houses of the sixteenth and seventeenth centuries. Robert Cecil, like his father, took a keen interest in architecture and might have dreamt up the basic design. After all it was an exercise in image building and status seeking in the game of politics and courtship. Certainly he employed Robert Lyminge, a carpenter-cum-architect, on the entrance front, and Simon Basil, Surveyor of the King's Works. Inigo Jones has also been associated with Hatfield, but without any documentary evidence.

Inside, one of the most impressive parts is the Marble Hall. This rises through two floors and is dressed with wooden wall panelling of exquisite craftsmanship. The fireplace is flanked by carved grotesque terms (sculpted posts) supporting an ornamental cornice, the type of feature found in a pattern book. At the upper end of the hall is a gallery which is a visual riot of carved strapwork panels surmounted by arched openings. Access to the upper floor is by the oak grand staircase. This is of the age when a stair changed from being merely a means of access to a place designed to create the expectation of splendours to come, by a show of the virtuosity of the woodcarver and the hanging of paintings on the walls.

Hardwick Hall is one of the earliest houses to have a grand staircase, but while it is spacious it is relatively austere compared to the elaborate wooden square newel type of which those at Knole, Kent, and Stonyhurst, Lancashire, pre-date Hatfield's by perhaps five years. At Hatfield, elaborately patterned newel posts support carvings of putti and monsters. A few steps up from the bottom, gates prevent dogs straying to the apartments above. These are divided into panels decorated with carved *fleurs-de-lis*.

No great house of the seventeenth century was without its long gallery: Hatfield's, directly over the loggia, ranks among the finest and remains unaltered. It is panelled throughout and has a ceiling of the most intricate strapwork. The two fireplaces are flanked by paired columns of alabaster on two levels in the manner of a triumphal gateway.

Robert Lyminge, who gave Hatfield its magnificent entrance front, also worked at Blickling Hall, Norfolk, and the church register of deaths at Blickling records him as 'the architect and builder of Blickling Hall'. Built originally for Sir Henry Hobart, the house is approached between two long wings of outbuildings containing the kitchens and stables. The house, in lovely red Norfolk brick, is then reached via a bridge across a dry moat. Its frontage is narrow, with a projected stone-arched porch flanked by Doric pilasters and crowned by an entablature. The bay window above is flanked by the Ionic order and has the conventional vertical mullions and horizontal transoms as in the windows at Hatfield. The brick entrance front is crowned by three Dutch gables; lead-capped brick stair turrets flank each corner. The triple-staged clock and belfry is also similar to that at Hatfield. Throughout there is a magnificent blend of reddish brick and stone dressing for windows, gables and quoining. Beyond the entrance, a small courtyard led to the Great Hall. This was considerably altered in the eighteenth century to become a hall for the grand staircase which is similar to that at Hatfield and therefore probably by Lyminge.

Blickling Hall,
Norfolk, 1616–25: one
of the most charming
examples of
seventeenth-century
brick domestic
architecture in England

The H plan was used at Charlton House, near Greenwich, for Sir Adam Newton, Secretary to Henry Prince of Wales. Not as large as Hatfield or Blickling, Charlton is also predominantly of red brick with stone reserved for windows, quoining, plat-bands, balustrade and the ornate centrepiece with arched porch. The plan of the house may have been by John Thorpe (1563–1655) to whom are attributed other Jacobean houses including Audley End. The magnificent stone centrepiece was borrowed from 'patterns' by the German, Wendel

Charlton Park, Wiltshire: a fine example of plaster strapwork with pendants, c. 1625

Dietterlin; such a riot of uninhibited classical distortion is also seen above the entrances to Bramshill, Hampshire and Aston Hall, Birmingham. Like Elizabethan Hardwick Hall, the hall is placed axially, that is across the body of the house, and so entered directly from the porch. Like Blickling, the roof line is broken by tall brick chimneys of elaborate patterning. Its Jacobean identity is firmly secured by the tall, lead-capped turrets placed to each side of the house.

Banqueting House,
Whitehall, London,
c. 1619–22: the only
surviving remnant of
Whitehall Palace

9

Inigo Jones

As we have seen, classical detail had been introduced into British architecture from the middle of the sixteenth century. However, it was Inigo Jones who first produced a scholarly interpretation of the classical style through his two visits to Italy and his deep study of the writings of Vitruvius, a 1st century AD Roman architect. Unfortunately, many of his plans did not get beyond the drawing-board due to expense or the political upheaval of the Civil War, or they may have been destroyed. With his greatness his name has inevitably been linked with buildings for which there is no documentary evidence of his involvement.

Inigo Jones was born in Smithfield, London, in 1573 but nothing is known of his education and training until 1603 when he is recorded in the Duke of Rutland's accounts as a 'picture maker'. By then he had made his first visit to Italy. He was employed at the court of James 1 as a designer of scenery and costumes for masques. Many drawings of these ambitious entertainments survive, showing moveable scenery and the first use of a proscenium arch. His earliest excursion into architecture may have been in 1608 with a design for a new Exchange for Merchants in the Strand, London. In 1611 he was appointed Surveyor to Prince Henry, heir to the throne. This post, involving the maintenance of all buildings and property owned or visited by the Prince, was short-lived due to Henry's premature death in 1613.

At this point Jones was invited to go on a second visit to Italy as artistic adviser to Thomas Howard, Earl of Arundel. This was to be most influential as Jones took a copy of Palladio's *Quattro Libri dell' architettura* which he may have purchased on his first visit. With this he diligently studied the buildings of Palladio in Vicenza as well as the antique remains of Rome. He was not, however, to become a slavish imitator of Palladio but an interpreter with due respect for other Italian masters as well.

On his return to England in 1615 he was appointed Surveyor to King James 1. He was also to hold the appointment during the reign of Charles 1 until the Civil War. His first major work and one which survives is the Queen's House, Greenwich. Built originally as two rectangular blocks on either

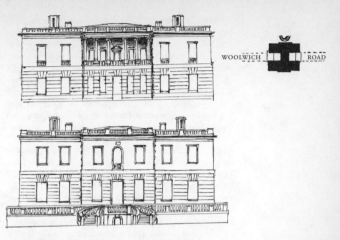

WOOLWICH   ROAD

side of the Woolwich Road and connected by a central bridge on the upper floor, it combines features from villas by Palladio and Sangallo without being a copy of any particular building. It is built of brick, faced in plaster and with the lower stage rusticated. Stone is reserved for the window architraves, cornices and Ionic pilasters of the loggia. A stone

Queen's House, Greenwich: plan shows addition of side bridges over Woolwich Road

balustrade hides the roof. Started for Anne of Denmark, wife of James I, it was completed for Henrietta Maria in 1637. However, its appearance was radically altered by John Webb in the 1660s with the addition of short connecting galleries on each side, and the addition of Doric colonnades in 1807 when it became a naval asylum.

Jones's next work and arguably his most formally classical was the Banqueting House, Whitehall (c. 1619–22). This building of double cube proportion is loosely derived from Palladio's Palazzo Barbarano, Vicenza, but Jones was not a copyist. The façade displays the Ionic and Corinthian orders, raised on a rusticated basement and crowned by a balustrade. The windows have the formality of Italian classicism with cornices over those on the lower floor and alternating triangular and semi-circular pediments on the upper. The centre of the façade is emphasised by half pillars and the end of the façade is closed by paired pilasters as was the manner of sixteenth-century Italian public buildings.

Jones was also responsible for the first example of formal town planning in Britain, that of Covent Garden, dating from the 1630s. Said to have been inspired by the piazza at Livorno, it certainly bore a close resemblance to the Place des Vosges, Paris

(c. 1605). On land leased from the Earl of Bedford, it comprised terraces over ground arcades on the eastern and northern sides while the west contained the church of St Paul. An eastern portico was of the Tuscan order, said by Vitruvius to be the most primitive of the classical orders. The terraces were of brick with plaster pilasters dividing the windows from each other. The idea of a ground-floor arcade was found not only in the Place des Vosges (formally Royale) but also in the Place Dauphin, c. 1607.

Jones's name has also been linked with the layout of the west side of Lincoln's Inn Fields, without documentary evidence, although the builder was probably Nicholas Stone who worked under Jones at the Banqueting House. Here we find the use of giant ordered pilasters and triangular pediments over the windows of the piano nobile.

As court architect Jones was responsible for the design of the Queen's Chapel, St James's Palace (1623–27), for Prince Charles's French Catholic bride Henrietta Maria and her retinue. It is austere externally with a Venetian window at the east end. Inside, a coffered barrel ceiling survives.

Another royal commission which did not go beyond the basic planning stage was the rebuilding of Whitehall Palace. Drawings survive in the hands of

Jones and his nephew John Webb showing a building which, if built, would have rivalled the Escorial in Madrid and the Louvre in Paris. The elevation of two major floors was to be broken at intervals by pavilions displaying the orders and formal entrances flanked by towers capped by domes.

Jones was also responsible for a major programme of restoration of St Paul's Cathedral. This included encasing the Gothic walls of the nave in a classical-style skin with semi-circular arches replacing the Gothic windows. At the western end he designed a huge Corinthian-ordered portico of ten columns based on Palladio's restoration of the antique Roman Temple of the Sun and Moon. This was flanked by two low towers, one (on the south side) incorporating the medieval towers of St Gregory the Great. Although the portico survived the Great Fire, it was demolished in 1687 as Wren's new cathedral arose.

We can obtain some idea of its appearance by looking at the west front of St John's church, Northampton (*c.* 1680), which must have been influenced by St Paul's.

Outside London, Jones has been associated with many country houses including Castle Ashby and Stoke Bruerne, Northamptonshire and Wilton, Wilt-

Queen's Chapel,
St James's Palace,
London:
c. 1623–27

shire. Stoke has the plan of a Palladian villa and was built for Sir Francis Crane who had established the tapestry factory at Mortlake near London. A central block was linked to the pavilions by curving colonnades. At Castle Ashby Jones may have advised on the addition of a gallery to link the two Tudor wings, thus enclosing a front court. Here he uses the Doric on the ground level and Ionic on the first stage pilasters and half pillars.

Jones's involvement in Wilton is hard to unravel. The south front was begun in about 1632 and is attributed to Isaac de Caus, possibly with Jones as consultant, as it has a similarity to detail in his design for the Prince's Lodging at Newmarket. It was severely damaged by fire in 1647 and restoration was put in the hands of John Webb. The restored interior includes the famous 'Cube' and 'Double Cube' room which is decorated in a rich Flemish-French manner although the doorcases are derived from those at Jones's Banqueting House.

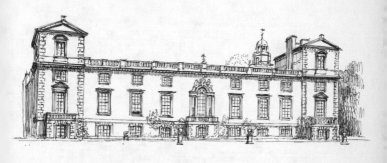

Wilton House,
Wiltshire: south front,
c. 1630

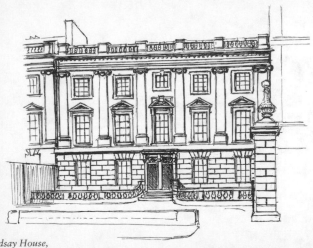

Lindsay House,
Lincoln's Inn Fields,
London: c. 1640

10

Seventeenth-Century Mannerism

Outside London the impact of the renaissance of classical architecture was varied. Much that passes within the term 'classical' was designed by masons and craftsmen, and even amateur gentlemen who had read foreign texts on architectural proportion and usage. Results varied from the absorption of the Whitehall court style of Jones and his circle to a mixture of styles from the Netherlands and France. The works of individual masons are not well documented. Nicholas Stone (1586–1647) has been linked with Lindsay House, Lincoln's Inn Fields, and the use of giant ordered pilasters. In the provinces one of the most notable masons was John Jackson of Oxford to whom is attributed the Baroque south porch of St Mary the Virgin (1637) and the Canterbury Quadrangle in St John's College (1632–36).

The former is a curious addition to the medieval church and shows the first use of twisted columns supporting the Corinthian order. Although such a feature had been used *c.* 1625 for the baldacchino in St Peter's, Rome, it is likely that Jackson's source was those depicted in a panel by Rubens in the Banqueting House ceiling. At St John's we find the east and west sides of the Canterbury Quadrangle filled by ranges supported over an arcade of Tuscan Doric pillars. The centrepieces of two stages have paired columns of the Doric and Ionic orders, surmounted by a semi-circular pediment. The east front has a bronze figure of Charles 1 by Hubert Le Sueur set into a niche flanked by Corinthian pillars and surmounted by a triangular pediment. The west side is identical except that the figure is of Queen Henrietta Maria. The upper stage of the range on either side, with rectangular windows with stone mullions and the battlemented parapet above, might seem to be a continuation of the collegiate style of the previous hundred years.

This reluctance to adopt the classical style at Oxford can be seen at Brasenose College. Here the chapel and library of about 1656–59 have windows filled with Gothic tracery set within walls divided by Corinthian-ordered pilasters and crowned with

*St John's College,
Oxford: Canterbury
Quadrangle*

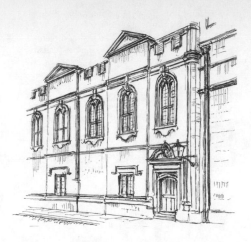

Brasenose College, Oxford, c. 1636–39: library frontage from Radcliffe Square showing the integration of classical features with the Gothic

pediments. The parapet is partially battlemented and adorned with pinnacles and urns. The inside of the chapel has a plaster fan and pendant vaulted ceiling. At Christ Church the Great Staircase to the dining hall has a remarkable fan vault of about 1640

126

in which most of the weight is supported on one central pier.

It was at Cambridge that the first complete college rebuilding was undertaken in the classical style, that of Clare, originally founded in 1338. The rebuilding began in 1638 with the east range and entrance to the court, and the west range facing the Fellows Garden and Backs in 1640. Work was interrupted by the Civil War and not resumed until the 1660s. The entrance includes triple orders, a rusticated arch and an oriel window projecting from the middle stage. The west range introduces giant Ionic-ordered pilasters dividing the façade into seven bays on either side of the gateway to the court, probably under the influence of the Jones-Webb circle and contemporary with Lindsay House and Lees Court. The balustrade is open so as to admit light to the roof dormers which are themselves adorned by alternating triangular and semi-circular pediments.

In order to facilitate the movement of building materials to the site, a bridge was built across the Cam between 1635–40. Designed by Thomas Grumbold, a Northamptonshire mason, it was strongly influenced by a design for a triple-arched bridge by Palladio in his *Quattro Libri*, with the substitution of a balustrade instead of a parapet.

*Clare College,
Cambridge, c. 1640:
west front*

Away from the academic environment of Oxford and Cambridge the reigns of James I and Charles I saw the building of a number of houses in a style that the late Sir John Summerson called 'Artisan Mannerism'. Since it was largely dependent on the adaptation of pattern-book detail, the result can be seen as quaint or unusual and certainly more reminiscent of the Low Countries than Italy. In the southern counties brick was used extensively: three outstanding

Dutch House, Kew, Surrey

Northern English diagonal window gables, with classical pediment above door, c. 1650

examples are Swakeleys near Uxbridge of about 1629, the so-called Dutch House at Kew of 1631, and Broome Park near Canterbury of about 1635.

Swakeleys and Broome are of pronounced H plan and Kew is basically rectangular. The principal distinguishing features of this style are the so-called Dutch gables adorning the roof line. The east and west façades of Broome are dressed with giant ordered brick pilasters, and the casement windows are retained. At Swakeleys stone is used for window cases, doorways, quoining at the wall angles and the framing of gables. At Kew the work is in brick throughout although the visual harmony has been somewhat marred by the replacement of mullioned casements with later sash windows. The centre is emphasised by an attempt to create the three orders in brick, even to the carving of Ionic and Corinthian capitals. The roof line of Kew is dominated by a battery of eight brick chimney stacks.

Dutch or Flemish gables were also used extensively in eastern England for farmhouses, barns and sheds, as well as almshouses. In northern England Dutch gables were rare. The traditional diagonal facing was retained and the only hint of classicism would have been the doorcase.

If stone was not ideal for a highly decorative translation of an engraved pattern book plate to the wall surface, plaster certainly was and the craft of pargetting (found principally in Suffolk) provides a rich variety of Flemish patterns including strapwork swags, naive figures and coats of arms. An outstanding example is Sparrows House, Ipswich.

The degree of classical influence in houses of the mid century varied from the heavily Italianate in buildings by or attributed to John Webb and his cir-

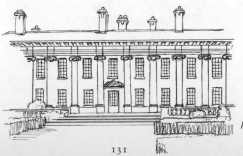

Lees Court, Kent, c. 1640: the roof may originally have been hidden behind a parapet

The Vyne, Hampshire: stone portico c. 1660

cle, to a Dutch Palladianism, a result of exile during the Commonwealth of builders in sympathy with the Stuart cause. Lees Court near Faversham, Kent (*c.* 1640), is an Italianate, long rectangular building dressed with giant Corinthian-ordered pilasters throughout its length. The roof is projected out over an eaves cornice of considerable depth supported by brackets. Perhaps this was influenced by the terraces of houses which had recently been built in London's Lincoln's Inn Fields and Great Queen Street with giant ordered pilasters running through the *piano nobile* and upper floor. At The Vyne, Hampshire, a house dating from the Tudor period, John Webb

made alterations to the interior as well as adding the first giant ordered portico of any house in England (*c.* 1660).

The Dutch influence in the second half of the seventeenth century is more formal to the extent that such buildings as the Dutch House at Kew are made to seem rather quaint. A feature that now appears is the hipped roof, sometimes balustraded and adorned

Ashdown House, Berkshire, c. 1650: rather Dutch in flavour with its hipped roof, balustrade and central cupola

in the centre by an octagonal lantern and cupola. A fine example is Ashdown House, Berkshire (*c.* 1650). This has been attributed to the Dutch-born Huguenot, Sir Balthazar Gerbier (1591–1667), since it was built for the Earl of Craven who commissioned Gerbier to build nearby Hampstead Marshall. Ashdown is virtually a cube of three floors above a basement divided by horizontal plat-bands. The hipped roof is boldly projected over eaves and the east and west fronts are pierced with triple dormers, while tall chimneys rise from the other two sides. The corners of the walls have quoining. In many respects it seems almost the prototype of the traditional doll's house.

Sadly one of the most famous houses of the mid-century decade, Coleshill (1650), not far from Ashdown, was destroyed by fire in 1952. It was designed by the gentleman architect Roger Pratt (1620–84) who had travelled on the continent during the Civil War and had stayed in Rome. It seems to have borne a resemblance to Newington House near Oxford (*c.* 1630), perhaps one of the earliest examples of a hipped roof and central cupola. Coleshill was a double-square in plan with a corridor running across the middle of the house on each floor, and rooms on either side justifying its label as a 'double-pile' house. Its harmony of detail was particularly pleasing. The façades were divided into three stages including basement. Ground and upper floors were divided by a plat-band. The wall surface was of ashlar with corner quoining. The nine windows on each floor were spaced into two narrow and one wide set corresponding with the hipped roof dormers. Pairs of chimneys rose from the slope of the roof, two at each side and two marking the longitudinal walls within and the corresponding broad space between each set of windows. The entrance led directly into the stair hall rising through the ground and upper floors. Directly opposite was the great parlour or salon and on the upper floor, entered from the gallery, was the great dining room. The basement contained the service rooms including a kitchen, pantry, larder, dairy, servants' hall and still room. Back stairs each side of the house linked the basement with the upper floors and servants' quarters in the roof. Thus servants were able to move about unseen.

Red or pinkish brick is always associated with Dutch architecture – Holland has no natural building stone. Therefore Eltham Lodge in south London (*c.* 1665) seems the quintessential Dutch house of the period. Like Coleshill, it is a double-pile but the grand stair has been moved to the centre of the house beyond the entrance hall. It was designed by Hugh

Squeries Court, Westerham, Kent, c. 1680: beautifully proportioned, even the recessed panelled brick chimneys add to its charm

May who became a leading figure at the Court of
Charles II and who had been in exile during the
Commonwealth, mainly in Holland. The influence of
Jacob van Campen's Mauritshuis at The Hague is
easily apparent but Eltham Lodge is far from being a
mere copy. On the north entrance front it has a giant
pilastered centrepiece with a pediment on a level with
the slope of the hipped roof. The windows on each
floor may be an early example of the sash type which
from now on gradually replaced casements. The sides
of the roof, pierced by dormers, project out over an
eaves cornice supported by small brackets (modil-
lions). From the flat of the roof rise four pairs of
brick chimney stacks with the added elegance of
recessed panels on each face.

Another fine example of the Anglo-Dutch style
of the Restoration is Ramsbury Manor, Wiltshire,
with a similar entrance front elevation to Eltham
Lodge. Here, however, the pedimental centrepiece is
slightly projecting, with corner quoining. As at
Eltham, the main pediment is adorned with a car-
touche and swags. Pilasters are not used. The main
floors are divided by a plat-band and the entrance
door is surmounted by a pediment. Squeries Court,
Westerham, Kent (c. 1680) for John Warde, son of a
Lord Mayor of London, also has a strong Dutch

flavour with the pinkish brick and hipped roof. It is also rectangular like Coleshill but one bay shorter on either side. A similar house to Squeries is nearby Tadworth Court, Surrey (c. 1694), with a centrepiece beneath a prominent pediment. It displays brickwork of the highest quality.

In the second half of the century the H plan of the Tudor and Jacobean period was again popular. Thus, the entrance front is flanked by projecting wings, at first minimal, as at Honington Hall, Warwickshire (c. 1671), although Groombridge Place, Kent (c. 1661), is a more definite H. One of the most impressive and influential versions was Clarendon House, Piccadilly (1664), by Roger Pratt, the architect of Coleshill, with which it had a distinct visual link. Built in brick, it had a slightly projected pedimented centrepiece. The side wings projected considerably. A balustraded hipped roof extended across the whole house, with a cupola in the centre. Although demolished in 1684, it was closely copied in William Winde's Belton House, Lincolnshire (1684–86), although on a smaller scale.

Perhaps the finest example of a country house of the period, Belton has a simple hall and salon division through the body with the main stair placed in a hall to one side. The walls of the principal rooms

are covered with exquisite panelling in oak and
walnut with highly naturalistic fruit and flower
carving by Grinling Gibbons and his school. The
high plaster ceilings are divided by deeply moulded
rectangular and elliptical panels, decorated with
flower mouldings.

The first half of the seventeenth century was not
one for major church building, after all there were
many redundant former religious houses now prey to
the needs of those seeking building stone. In many
instances it was a question of alteration rather than

*Belton House,
Lincolnshire,
c. 1684–86*

Staunton Harold, Leicestershire: church with porch, c. 1653. A perfect integration of latent Gothic with Mannerist pattern-book classicism

rebuilding, such as the introduction of a pulpit and family pews or a carved screen. One of the first churches built following the Reformation was that of Groombridge, Kent (1623), in the Perpendicular style. This was also the style of the largest church of the period, St John's, Leeds (1632–33). In London, St Katherine Cree (c. 1631) is a mixture of classical and Gothic. The interior has semi-circular arcading resting on Corinthian-ordered pillars. The clerestory is Perpendicular, the east window of the chancel reminiscent of window tracery in old St Paul's Cathedral. The vault is almost flat, forming a star-patterned decoration incorporating large heraldic bosses. In 1631 Inigo Jones's St Paul's Covent Garden was begun as part of the development of the Earl of Bedford's land, and here we see a primitive Tuscan Doric for the portico and austere brickwork for the sides.

Church building virtually ceased during the Commonwealth although one rare example was built in stark defiance of Cromwell. This is the Perpendicular church of Staunton Harold, Leicestershire, begun in 1653. It is only when one comes close to the west door beneath the tower that one is confronted by the most amazing mixture of classical Mannerist and Baroque ornament. The arched door is flanked by tapering paired pilasters linked by swags, Flemish in flavour. Above the entablature, tall statues of angels flank a framed inscription which tells us that the founder, Sir Robert Shirley, did 'ye best things in ye worst times'. For this noble action he went to the Tower of London.

Apart from the rebuilding of the City of London churches after the Great Fire, major church building did not start again until the eighteenth century, by which time Britain had absorbed the Baroque and was on the verge of Palladianism.

11

Sir Christopher Wren

(1632–1723)

The name Wren is synonymous with the rebuilding of St Paul's Cathedral, a building which elevates his status to that of a major architect to stand alongside his continental contemporaries. His achievements were for the most part due to the unfortunate circumstances of the Great Fire of London in 1666; without this he is unlikely to have become Surveyor of the King's Works, an appointment he held for over 40 years, and would probably have remained in academic appointments in Oxford.

He was born the son of the rector of East Knoyle in Wiltshire. His father was soon elevated to the deanery of Windsor and thus he was brought up in an atmosphere of pronounced royal leanings. He was sent to Westminster School and entered Wadham College Oxford in 1649. Here he excelled as a natural scientist; John Evelyn the diarist called him 'that miracle of youth'. Upon graduation he remained a lecturer in mathematics until 1657, when he was appointed to the Gresham Professorship in Astronomy in London. In 1661 he was appointed Savilian Professor of Astronomy at Oxford and in the same year was a Foundation Member of the Royal Society.

His turning to architecture was perhaps unusual for someone who had not studied the great masters of the Renaissance at first hand. In 1661 he was brought to the notice of King Charles II as an able draughtsman through his illustrations of the *Cerebri Anatome* of fellow Oxford scientist Dr Willis. Appearing to the king as a man of great practical ability, he was invited to take charge of the fortifications of Tangiers (part of the marriage dowry of Charles's wife, Catherine of Braganza). This he declined, perhaps on the grounds of ill health, and remained in Oxford where he was soon approached to design a building for university ceremonies. This is the Sheldonian Theatre, named after the then Bishop of London and former Warden of All Souls' College, Gilbert Sheldon.

To fulfil its purpose, the building needed as wide a space as possible unencumbered by piers supporting the roof. The inspiration for the ground plan was the antique Theatre of Marcellus, known from engravings in Serlio's treatise on architecture. The exterior is relatively plain with a formal entrance between Corinthian half columns on the wide south front. The interior has seats ranked in steps round the central auditorium. Further seating is set in a circular wooden gallery painted to simulate marble. Light is admitted through segmented windows beneath the gallery and a clerestory above. The most ingenious part of the structure is the timber roof construction with each truss dovetailed together to form triangular supports for the roof above and flat support for the painted roof panels beneath. These are painted to represent the open sky above a folded *velarium* or canvas awning. The joints of the panels are hidden behind wooden beading moulded and painted to simulate rope.

In 1663 Wren was appointed a member of the Commission for the repair of St Paul's Cathedral which had suffered at the hands of the Parliamentarians, as well as awaiting completion of the restoration started by Inigo Jones. His proposals included the reconstruction of the crossing area with a dome supported on eight piers to replace the rather squat square tower. His initial inspiration probably came from an engraving of Bramante's dome for St Peter's in his copy of Serlio. The plague in 1665 gave Wren the opportunity to visit France (the only time he travelled abroad). Most of his time was spent in Paris, and by chance the greatest master of the Italian Baroque, Gianlorenzo Bernini, was there to design an east front for the Louvre. They actually met but 'the old reserved Italian gave me but a few Minutes of his time' (Wren, in a letter to the Reverend Dr Bateman on his activities in Paris).

He studied the Louvre in detail, visited Versailles just before the expansion under Levau and J H Mansart, and numerous other great houses. St Paul's must have been uppermost in his mind and so he would have paid particular attention to the churches of the Sorbonne by Jacques Lemercier, and Val-de-Grâce by François Mansart and Lemercier. These in turn were influenced by churches in Rome such as Il Gesu and had domes raised on drums over the crossing. The sight of these and an engraving of St Peter's, Rome, with the dome completed after a design by Michelangelo must have reinforced Wren's desire to make a radical break with tradition.

Wren submitted his report on the proposed restoration to the Commission in May 1666 along with detailed elevations in pen and wash in his own hand. The opening out of the crossing space from a square to an octagon may have been suggested by that of Ely Cathedral where his uncle, Matthew, had been bishop. The dome raised upon a tall drum owes much to Michelangelo although the introduction of an inner dome connected to a lantern rising through the outer dome shell was close to Lemercier's church of the Sorbonne. Finally the lantern was to be capped by a pineapple-shaped steeple.

Wren could hardly have known how fortunate he was going to be when just six days after the approval of his plan the Great Fire swept across the City of London between 2 and 6 September.

With three-quarters of the City destroyed, a Commission was immediately set up to address the problem of rebuilding. By 11 September Wren had produced a plan introducing broad thoroughfares between a civic centre and St Paul's, intersected by a grid pattern of minor streets. It combined something of the grandeur of Sixtus v's Rome and Henri iv's Paris. Unfortunately, the need to get the City functioning as quickly as possible had to come before Wren's proposal of a total rebuilding, which was in any case beyond the financial means of Parliament, City merchants and the Crown. Wren's contribution was to be limited to the rebuilding of 53 parish churches, St Paul's Cathedral and the Customs

St Paul's Cathedral: pre-fire dome design, c. 1666

House. In 1669 he was appointed Surveyor of Works and he resigned his academic position as Savilian Professor at Oxford in 1671.

Although Wren had been working on plans for the rebuilding of St Paul's since the fire, work did not start until 1675. Work on the churches began immediately after the Rebuilding Act of 1670, which also imposed a tax on coal shipped to London to help raise a steady income. Although it is popularly assumed that he designed all the churches himself this is not quite true. Increasingly scholars attribute work to Dr Robert Hooke, a fellow Oxford mathematician, and Edward Woodroffe who had been Surveyor to the Dean and Chapter of Westminster. Wren must have deputed work in much the same way that artists left minor parts of a painting to pupils. Some have even suggested that Wren designed little more than the towers in any detail

*St Benet's,
Paul's Wharf, 1677–83*

and since many of these were not built until the end of the century, they may owe much to the hand of Nicholas Hawksmoor who had come to London to enter Wren's office as scholar and domestic clerk in 1679.

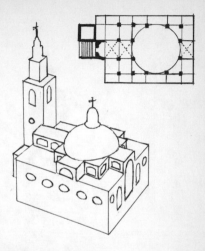

No two churches are alike and they are masterpieces of original planning on a confined scale. Some are of the columned basilican plan, such as St Bride, or a simple box like St Benet, Paul's Wharf. Others, such as St Stephen Walbrook, incorporate a dome. The richer parishes rebuilt in Portland stone although many churches had bodies constructed in red brick, stone being reserved for the window surrounds, corner quoining and towers. These would incorporate a belfry stage dressed with classical pilasters and surmounted by steeples, the most famous being those of St Bride and St Mary le Bow. Internal fittings were

St Stephen Walbrook

St Mary le Bow,
1670–80
St Magnus the Martyr,
1671–76 (steeple
c. 1705)
St Dunstan in the East,
1670–71 (steeple
c. 1697)

carved by Grinling Gibbon and his assistants. The moulded plasterwork was also of exceptionally high quality.

Design ideas can be traced to various sources including Italian Baroque for the tower of St Vedast, Forster Lane, and Dutch for the external brick treatment of St Benet and the internal cross-vaulted plans of St Anne and St Agnese, and St Martin, Ludgate, perhaps influenced by the strong interest in Dutch architecture of Wren's colleague Hooke. The tower of St Magnus the Martyr bears a strong likeness to that of St Charles Borromeo in Antwerp. The rusticated and recessed entrance to St Mary le Bow has a striking likeness to François Mansart's design for the entrance to the Hôtel de Conté, Paris. The coffered dome of St Stephen, Walbrook is a simplified version of contemporary Roman examples but on a circular rather than an oval plan.

(A century later, S. P. Cockerell was to use the idea of a circular dome supported on eight Corinthian columns within a square nave at St Mary, Banbury, Oxfordshire.)

The story of the rebuilding of St Paul's is com-

St Martin, Ludgate,
1672–84

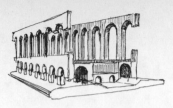

plex, not least because hundreds of drawings from Wren's office survive, some in his own hand, but many are the work of assistants and are undated. The fact that the completed building differs so much from the Warrant design of 1675 begs the question as to when he fixed on the final version, or did he re-design parts and details throughout the 35-year building campaign? How much did Wren leave to his able assistants, Edward Woodroffe, Joshua Marshall and Thomas Strong? This should in no way reduce the part Wren played but rather emphasise the support and trust of a close-knit office of work.

Until 1668 the Commission for rebuilding the City believed that old St Paul's could be restored. However, with the collapse of a nave pier Dean Sancroft commissioned Wren, who was still in Oxford, to provide designs for a new building, the cost to be borne by the tax on coal. In 1670 Wren produced a

OPPOSITE *St Stephen, Walbrook, 1672–79*

ABOVE *Wooden model for St Paul's Cathedral, c. 1670*

153

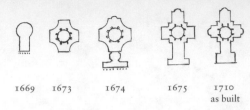

wooden model in the form of a rectangular hall with
side chambers or loggias to provide space for busi-
ness. At the western end was to be a square section
surmounted by a dome.

In 1673 he produced the so-called Greek Cross
plan which he must have derived from a knowledge
of Michelangelo's ideas for a centralised St Peter's,
François Mansart's design for a Bourbon chapel of St
Denis near Paris, and a drawing by John Webb for a
'Greek Cross church'. At the centre rose a dome resting on eight piers.

The following year the Great Model appeared.
This incorporated the Greek Cross design but with a
western extension to include a domed vestibule and
giant Corinthian-ordered portico reminiscent of the
Pantheon in Rome. The wooden model remains for

*St Paul's Cathedral:
development of plan*

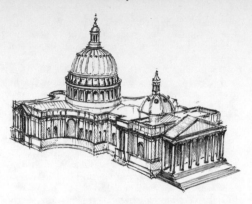

us today in the crypt of St Paul's and allows us to see the detail that was intended for the interior, with Corinthian pilasters placed against the eight piers. Light was to be admitted through large windows in the concave walls to the ambulatory circling the dome while light would come directly into the central area from the drum beneath the dome. Some have suggested that had it been built it would have been rather dark due to the narrowness of the openings between the piers. Unfortunately this design, which

St Paul's Cathedral: the Great Model, 1674

was said to be Wren's favourite, was rejected by the Commission on the grounds of cost, practicality and its radical departure from the traditional Latin Cross form.

Some time between its rejection in autumn 1674 and April 1675 Wren produced what is known as the Warrant design which returned to the traditional plan, and included a western portico similar to that Inigo Jones built against the old cathedral in 1635. It is tempting to think of this plan as being an early post-fire idea and hardly a serious intention of Wren's, with an extraordinary saucer supporting a tall Michelangelesque drum and dome. Above this is a tall steeple reminiscent of that to be built later at St Bride. In granting the royal warrant for construction the king was pleased to allow Wren 'the liberty in the prosecution of his work, to make variations, rather ornamental than essential, as from time to time he should see proper' (14 May 1675). So this was an invitation to Wren to build a masterpiece as he saw fit.

Since drawings, sometimes referred to as the Penultimate design and perhaps dating from before the end of 1675, exist and bear a striking resemblance at least to the detail of the elevation of the nave as built, it is likely that Wren finalised much of

St Paul's Cathedral

the design within a few months of the royal warrant. The elevation includes the upper storey screen wall which hides the buttressing of the clerestory wall behind and adds greater strength to the external appearance. This fundamental alteration to the design could not be carried out before the laying of adequate foundations to absorb the additional load. Indeed, the site was being cleared for the 'setting out' of the foundations in 1673. This applied also to the foundations for the crossing piers which were obviously intended to support a heavier structure than that shown in the Warrant drawings, and similar in scale to the dome in the Penultimate design.

Work commenced in June 1675 and by 1697 the quire was complete. The nave and west front followed by 1708, and the dome between about 1706 and the completion of the cathedral in 1710. The final result is a triumph of proportion, the dome and drum rising majestically. The style may be designated as English High Renaissance or muted Baroque. It has articulation derived from Jones's Banqueting House, transeptal porticoes inspired by Cortona in Rome, west front with a gallery of paired Corinthian columns from Perrault and Levau at the Louvre, and west towers of Borromini flavour. The dome owes a debt to both Michelangelo and Bramante.

Only by exploring the cathedral can we fully understand and admire Wren's inventiveness which combined his skill as an architectural designer with engineering. The dome we see from outside is no more than a lead shell. The lantern is supported on a brick and stone cone which merges with an inner dome, the combined load then transmitted through pendentives to eight piers.

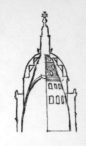

This allowed for an inner dome which did not create the effect of a funnel due to its height above the floor while the exterior dome was high enough to act as a focus and landmark from a distance. Wren had perhaps followed J H Mansart's dome construction on the chapel of Les Invalides in Paris. In order to increase the visual bulk of the nave and quire, as well as to hide flying buttresses which were considered unseemly for a classical building, Wren introduced false walls to the upper stage, dressed with paired pilasters and niches crowned with pediments.

In spite of Wren's work on the City churches and St Paul's, he was involved in the design of many other buildings in the later seventeenth century. At the two universities these include Pembroke College Chapel, Emmanuel College Chapel and Trinity College Library, Cambridge, and Tom Tower, Christ Church, Oxford. Royal contracts included a Palace of Win-

St Paul's Cathedral: dome section

chester (only partially finished and turned into a barracks in the nineteenth century), the conversion of Nottingham House, Kensington, for King William III and Queen Mary, apartments for Queen Mary at Whitehall Palace (burnt down in 1698), and the king and queen's apartments at Hampton Court where we see the domestic, human scale of English royal building contrasting with the overwhelming grandeur of contemporary Versailles.

Fortunately, royal funds did not run to reconstructing the whole Tudor palace so Wren was confined to the south-east corner. Here the apartments are built round the Fountain Court in pinkish-red brick with Portland stone window architraves and centrepieces along each front.

Wren probably advised on many projects for which no documentary evidence survives: buildings attributed to him include Morden College in Blackheath, Groombridge Place in Kent, and Winslow Hall in Buckinghamshire. This would be expected from an architect with many pupils and assistants.

His grandest domestic work was Greenwich Hospital in which he overcame the problem of relating the buildings to the earlier palace block by John Well and Inigo Jones's Queen's House. It should be admired from the Isle of Dogs with the blocks and colonnades receding so as to draw the eye back to the Queen's House.

Wren was forced to resign the office of Surveyor of Work in 1718 as opportunities were given to younger men. His City was rebuilt, his cathedral complete, but the Baroque style was now being superseded by the austere Palladian movement. Wren died at the age of 91 in 1723 and was buried in the crypt of St Paul's Cathedral. *Lector, si monumentum requiris circumspice.*

12

The Baroque Style

In an architectural context the term Baroque is associated with the Roman Catholic Counter Reformation and the spiritual zeal of the Church in Italy and central Europe in the seventeenth century. It invokes visions of highly ornamented façades and a sense of movement created by a flow of concave and convex surfaces, of interiors in which illusions of heavenly or courtly grandeur are created by the merging of architectural forms into indefinite space. Gianlorenzo Bernini and Francesco Borromini are the supreme architects and Giovanni Battista Gaulli and Andrea Pozzo the masters of painterly illusion.

Nowhere in Protestant Britain do we approach the architectural complexities of, for instance, Borromini's St Ivo or Bernini's St Andrea al Quirinale, although in Baroque painted interiors there is more feeling of being part of an arm of the continental movement. After all the Italian master Antonio Verrio decorated apartments at Chatsworth and Burghley, and

OPPOSITE *St John, Smith Square, Westminster, 1714–28*

James Thornhill painted the apotheosis of William and Mary on the ceiling of the Great Hall of Greenwich Hospital, on a grander scale than anything Charles Lebrun did for Louis XIV at Versailles. Certainly Andrea Pozzo, the creator of the architectural *trompl'oeil* ceiling of St Ignazio, Rome, would have approved of Thornhill's ceiling at Moor Park, Hertfordshire, or the surprisingly little-known interior of St Lawrence, Whitchurch, Little Stanmore.

In architecture there are certainly continental Baroque influences such as Wren's borrowing of windows from Bernini's Palazzo Barbarino for the west front of St Paul's, or Thomas Archer's towers at St John, Smith Square, Westminster from Borromini's St Agnese in the Piazza Navona. While concave and convex surfaces or the interplay of staggered columns or pilasters on a church frontage proclaim the style in Italy from the early seventeenth century, there was really only a brief space of about 20 years at the beginning of the eighteenth century which witnesses something of a Baroque movement in Britain. Unlike on the continent, here it was heavy and austere with a vigorous modelling of contrasting parts or masses into blocks.

While Wren is often regarded as of the Baroque, he is more an architect of the period than the style.

Talman, Hawksmoor, Gibbs, Vanbrugh, and Archer are considered more 'complete' masters, particularly Archer and Gibbs who had the benefit of a late Baroque architectural education in Rome. William Talman (1650–1719) may be considered to have been the first Baroque architect of the country house and his south and west fronts of Chatsworth House between 1687 and 1702 introduce a classical grandeur new to domestic architecture. Inspired by one of Bernini's designs for the east front of the Louvre, the façades are raised on a rusticated basement. The west front is dressed with giant Corinthian pilasters and a projected pedimented centrepiece of giant half columns. The south front is dressed at both sides by giant pilasters and formality is further emphasised by the entablature and balustrade.

Hawksmoor's early years are rather in the shadow of Wren under whom he started his architectural

Chatsworth House, Derbyshire: west front

HORA E SEMPRE

Easton Neston,
Northamptonshire:
south or entrance front

career as 'Scholar and Domestic Clerk'. He worked at St Paul's Cathedral, Chelsea Hospital, Kensington Palace and Greenwich Hospital. His first independent commission was probably that of Easton Neston, Northamptonshire (*c.* 1699–1702), a house that seems to be strongly reminiscent of Talman's work at Chatsworth in the use of giant orders, although here they are of ashlar and not fluted. It also has a similarity to the King William block of Greenwich Hospital, possibly designed by Hawksmoor as well. The grand entrance front projects out in stages to an entrance which at first may seem almost visually crushed by the giant Corinthian half pillars. Above the projected entablature is a carved coat of arms of the patron Sir William Fermor, set against a semicircular headpiece.

Although Hawksmoor designed much of the detail at Castle Howard and Blenheim, the commissions were given to John Vanbrugh (1664–1726), to whom the basic designs are also attributed. Both were built more for effect than convenience and Vanbrugh, being of a romantic disposition and without too great a concern for cost, was the ideal person to create these expressions of power and grandeur. His background, on the other hand, seemed unlikely for such a successful architect. First a soldier, even arrested in France on a charge of spying, he had the pleasure of a short stay in the Bastille. On his return to England he left the army for the stage and wrote ten very successful plays including *The Relapse* and *The Provok'd Wife*. He was a Whig by inclination and a member of the Kit Kat Club. It was there in 1699 that he probably met Charles Howard, 3rd Earl of Carlisle, who gave him the commission, originally offered to William Talman, to design a new home to replace the Howard family seat of Henderskelfe Castle, recently destroyed by fire. Talman's charges were too high and his personality unpleasant and pretentious. Vanbrugh had the sense to seek the assistance of Hawksmoor who may have been recommended by Wren.

Castle Howard was planned as a domed central block with flanking side wings forming a wide garden front on the south. The north or entrance front was to be flanked by projecting wings at right angles for the kitchens and stables. The result was to have been totally symmetrical, and with the dominating central domed block linked by quadrants to the side wings may have been inspired by one of Wren's rejected plans for Greenwich Hospital.

The entrance front looks heavy and austere with rusticated courses and giant Doric ordered pilasters. The south or garden front is raised up on a rusticated basement throughout its length. While the central block is emphasised by height, the salon is marked by a projected pedimented centrepiece. The stonework is ashlar but each window is flanked by fluted Corinthian pilasters running the entire length of the front.

The entrance from the north leads directly into the hall which rises through the house to the drum and

Castle Howard,
Yorkshire:
the garden front

dome, supported on four huge piers. The drama is reinforced by shafts of light from the drum as well as through the arches between the piers, truly a hint of the theatrical. It is only after some moments that the true scale registers on the mind as we notice the fireplaces on either side of the hall. Beyond the hall is the salon facing out over the terrace and formal garden. On either side of the salon is an *enfilade* or line of rooms with a sequence of doors in alignment, which in effect creates a corridor through the apartments as at Chatsworth, deriving from the French layouts of Vaux le Vicomte and Versailles. The central block with flanking lower wings and the kitchen block were finished according to the original plan; however, the stable block was moved away from the house and its intended position occupied by the library wing built in the 1750s by William Robinson.

At Blenheim, commissioned in 1705 by John Churchill, 1st Duke of Marlborough, Vanbrugh and Hawksmoor created a mansion covering about seven acres. It is a mighty assertion of power and the gift of a 'grateful nation' to one who had clipped the power of Louis XIV, a bust of whom is set above the portico of the garden front. We enter via a huge court flanked by the kitchen and stable blocks, the majesty being intensified by the gradual closing together of

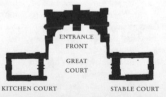

ENTRANCE
FRONT

GREAT
COURT

KITCHEN COURT

STABLE COURT

Blenheim Palace, Oxfordshire: the monumentality and grandeur of Versailles, but on a slightly smaller scale. The curving colonnades draw the eye into the magnificent entrance portico

Blenheim Palace: the stable block

the projecting blocks and colonnades. Entry is up two flights of steps and beneath a huge Corinthian portico of truly Roman grandeur. Inside the hall we see how the admission of light is heavily dependent on the introduction of an attic stage instead of a drum and dome as at Castle Howard. The ceiling was painted by Thornhill and depicts the Glorification of the Duke of Marlborough. Beyond in the salon is a remarkable illusion of space created by the *trompl'oeil* paintings of the peoples of the four continents looking into the room from between a row of columns. Painted by the French artist Louis Laguerre (who was cheaper than Thornhill), it was quite deliberately based on the wall decoration of the now-destroyed Ambassadors' Staircase at Versailles. The painted marble of the columns and balustrade merge with that of the doorcases and rusticated marble dado.

From the gardens the façades provide a balance between warm areas of Oxfordshire ashlar and the striking rusticated blocks of the corner towers surmounted by a heavy cornice and attic stage or 'eminence', generally attributed to Hawksmoor. The kitchen and stable blocks on either side of the entrance court occupy an area greater than that of many mansions. On a bleak day they look like prison blocks but on close analysis they are full of Vanbrugh

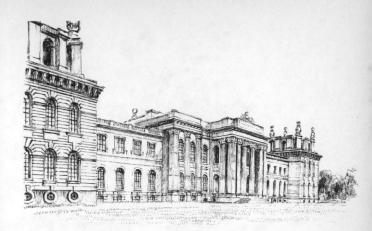

*Blenheim Palace:
the garden front*

whimsy. For instance, the entrance to the stable block is flanked by heavy paired Tuscan columns and entablature supporting nothing more than British lions crushing French cockerels. The towers are imaginative creations of two stages pierced by Vanbrughian arches.

Vanbrugh alone was responsible for Seaton Delaval, Northumberland (1721–28), and Grimsthorpe Castle, Lincolnshire. Although much smaller, Seaton has a similar basic layout to Blenheim. The entrance court is flanked by stable and kitchen blocks but the central block seems almost oppressive in its weight. The order is Doric and the paired columns on either side of the door are supported by a bevelled rusticated basement. The interior of the entrance hall has arcades of blind arches set into the walls. Grimsthorpe, also from the 1720s, is the transformation of a sixteenth-century quadrangular house, and exhibits elements from Blenheim and Seaton including paired rusticated Doric columns, arcading and block corner towers.

Hawksmoor's most original contributions are the six London churches constructed as a result of the 1711 Act for Fifty New Churches. Built in stone, and rectangular in plan, they all have an austere simplicity. Heavy keystones over windows, thick doorcases

OPPOSITE
*Seaton Delaval,
Northumberland,
1722–28*

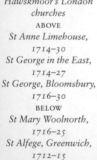

Hawksmoor's London churches
ABOVE
*St Anne Limehouse,
1714–30
St George in the East,
1714–27
St George, Bloomsbury,
1716–30*
BELOW
*St Mary Woolnorth,
1716–25
St Alfege, Greenwich,
1712–15*

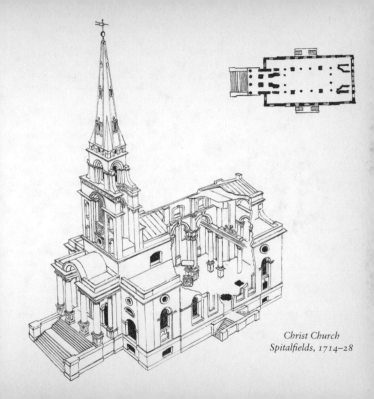

Christ Church
Spitalfields, 1714–28

and a variety of tower designs rival those of Wren.

Thomas Archer (1668–1743) was the most Baroque of British architects, having spent some years in Rome. His first commission, the church of St Philip, Birmingham (1709–15), invokes Borromini in the concave surfaces of the tower. At St Paul, Deptford, south Lonson (1712–30), the semi-circular entrance portico is reminiscent of Pietro da Cortona's work. St John, Smith Square (1714–28), has two gigantic porticoes *in antis* surmounted by broken roof pediments; the four corner towers again derive from Borromini. Archer's mansion for the Duke of Shrewsbury, Heythrop, has the powerful character of Bernini's design for the Louvre front but detail such as broken pediments reversed over pilasters is again Borromini. At Wrest Park, Bedfordshire, he designed a remarkable domed banqueting house largely in brick on the plan of a hexagon with round and square projections on alternate sides.

*Wrest Park,
Bedfordshire: the
banqueting house,
c. 1709*

It is hard to label James Gibbs (1682–1754) as a true Baroque architect; his work varies from the spirit of Roman Baroque to the austerity of the Palladian movement. In his church of St Mary le Strand, London (1714–17), he consciously invokes detail from his master, Carlo Fontana. Rectangular in plan and of two stages raised over a crypt, the sides are divided into bays by pilasters: Ionic (lower) and Corinthian (upper). On the upper stage each alternate bay is crowned by a triangular or semi-circular pediment creating an effect of movement. The tower in receding stages is set over a Wren-like belfry stage. His nearby St Martin-in-the-Fields (1721–26) resembles an antique temple from the front with its hexastyle Corinthian portico virtually masking the church behind. The sides are adorned with giant ordered Corinthian pilasters and windows surrounded by alternate courses of projected blocks, the so-called 'Gibbs' surround'. The east façade is adorned with a Venetian window, a major Palladian feature.

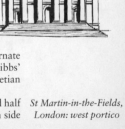

*St Martin-in-the-Fields,
London: west portico*

The interior has retained side galleries raised half the height of the nave pillars to allow light from side

St Martin-in-the-Fields
OPPOSITE *east front*
ABOVE *interior*

Radcliffe Camera,
Oxford

aisle windows. The sanctuary is flanked by side vestries and lit by a Venetian arch. The nave has a barrel-vaulted ceiling with delicate plaster decoration by the Italian stuccoists Artari and Bagutti, imported by Gibbs.

At All Saints, Derby (now Derby Cathedral), 1723–25, Gibbs modelled the interior closely on that of St Martin-in-the-Fields.

The steeple of St Martin-in-the-Fields is the most Baroque feature of all and was clearly reproduced a few years later by Henry Flitcroft at nearby St Giles in the Fields, as well as churches in the eastern states of America. In Glasgow in the 1740s, Allan Dreghorn produced a passable if somewhat heavy likeness to St Martin's in his St Andrew's church.

Gibbs's most dramatic building is the Radcliffe Camera, Oxford (1739–49), a development of a plan by Hawksmoor. Raised on a 16-sided rusticated base, a circular drum wall adorned with paired Corinthian pilasters supports an inner drum and a lead-covered dome and lantern. Powerful in its bulk, it commands attention, as does the domical bulk of Santa Maria della Salute, Venice. However, with the current of restraint running through the English Baroque movement, it stops short of the highly ornate volutes and obelisks of its Venetian counterpart.

*Stourhead, Wiltshire,
c. 1725: a perfectly
proportioned Palladian
mansion with a
frequently copied four-
columned Corinthian
portico. The wings were
added later*

13

The Palladian Movement

The full impact and scale of Baroque could never be imposed on a northern European Protestant nation where in any case there was not the patronage of a pope, doge or emperor. By the early eighteenth century, crown patronage and expenditure was limited by parliament so a royal building campaign like, for example, that of Louis XIV in France was out of the question. With the completion of the state apartments at Hampton Court in about 1705, large-scale royal building was over until George IV as Prince Regent commissioned Brighton Pavilion from John Nash in the oriental style.

The revolt against the so-called Baroque started in about 1715 and was almost as much about politics as taste. The Baroque was associated with the High Church, the Tory Party and the House of Stuart. It was essentially a Whig artistic movement although it also had a strong literary foundation. The Baroque had been seen by the Whig politician Lord Shaftesbury in 1712 in his 'Letter concerning the Art or Science of Design' as a frivolous and false style. In a veiled attack on Wren he wrote, 'Thro' several reigns we have patiently seen the noblest publick Buildings perish … under the Hand of one single Court Architect'.

Wren was now 70 and although he remained Surveyor of Works until 1718, he had been pushed into the background on the completion of St Paul's.

In their search for a pure architectural style, the Whigs were helped by the publication of two books in 1715 which extolled the virtues of Palladio as the architectural 'truth' and Inigo Jones as his disciple. The first of these, *Vitruvius Britannicus* by the Scottish architect Colen Campbell, was a survey of classical architecture in England from Jones to the present, interspersed with a few of Campbell's own proposals including his design for a great new London church to rival Wren's St Paul's. It was published in three volumes which, while clearly preaching a visual message of classical purity, nonetheless included engravings of the principal works of Baroque masters such as Wren, Vanbrugh, Hawksmoor and Archer. Their names were also included in the list of subscribers along with a dedication to George I. That Jones was Campbell's hero is made explicit in this statement: 'When those designs he gave Whitehall are published ... I believe all Mankind will agree with me, that there is no palace in the world to rival it'.

The second publication to give direction to the movement was Palladio's *Quattro Libri dell' architettura*, translated fully into English for the first time by Giacomo Leoni, a Venetian, and Nicholas Dubois, an Englishman of French extraction. Hitherto English architects had used or consulted editions in French or the original Italian. The Leoni and Dubois translation went through several revisions culminating in that by Isaac Ware in 1738 in which the copper engravings were accurate copies of the original woodcuts in Palladio's work. In 1743 an English translation of Palladio's *L'antichità di Roma* appeared.

With Campbell praising Jones's faithfulness to Palladio's architectural principles, it was not long before Jones's drawings were published in folios by William Kent (1727), Isaac Ware (1735) and John Vardy (1744). In 1728 Robert Castell published *Villas of the Ancients*, a series of reconstructions of Roman houses based on classical literature. Lord Burlington, who along with Campbell was to be the leading disciple of the movement, published *Fabbriche antiche* in 1730, a series of Palladio's drawings specially engraved from the originals in his possession.

While the movement rejected Baroque extravagance and over-ornamentation it does not mean that Palladian buildings were necessarily austere. Some were extremely grand – the entrance hall at Holkham can hardly be described as anything less than magnificent. The first building in this style was Wilbury House, Newton Tony, Wiltshire (1710), by William Benson, modelled on nearby Amesbury by Inigo Jones's nephew John Webb, but it was Colen Campbell (1676–1729) who was the leading architect of the movement.

Campbell was a lawyer by training but had turned his mind to architecture, designing a house for one of his clan in Glasgow in 1712. With the union with England in 1707 he, like many fellow Scots, saw London as the cultural and social centre of Britain and moved to the capital in search of commissions. Wisely committing himself to the Whig Party and the Hanovarian succession, he launched his *Vitruvius Britannicus* in the hope of establishment and success. By the time of the publication of the first volume in 1715 he had already been commissioned by Sir Richard Child, heir to an East India Company fortune, to design Wanstead House, Essex. The first version, subsequently rejected by Child, was published in volume one. As finally built, Wanstead consisted of a large rectangular block flanked by lower wings, some

90 metres (260 feet) long. Originally intended to have a cupola over the centre, it bore a slight likeness to Castle Howard, but without the pilaster divisions throughout its length. It was demolished in 1822.

Wanstead became the prototype for a number of Palladian mansions, including Prior Park near Bath and Wentworth Woodhouse in Yorkshire. A feature of each is the huge hexastyle (six-columned) portico raised above a rusticated basement. This was a feature of a number of Palladio's villas. The windows of the main floor were capped by triangular and semicircular pediments. The roof was contained behind a balustraded parapet.

One must question how Campbell had absorbed Palladio's vocabulary and detail. Not only must he have been acquainted with an Italian or French edition of Palladio's *Quattro Libri*, but he had visited Italy some time prior to 1715. This is evident from an unexecuted design for a *villa rotonda*, perhaps for Chiswick Park, the estate of Lord Burlington for whom Campbell worked after publication of *Vitruvius Britannicus*. The famous Villa Rotonda outside Vicenza also inspired James Smith, then Scotland's leading architect, to produce a design based on it.

It was not however in Scotland or at Chiswick that the closest interpretation of the Villa Rotonda is

to be found, but at Mereworth, Kent, where Campbell built a villa for John Fane, later Earl of Westmoreland, in 1722–23. It is square in plan with a hexastyle Ionic-ordered portico on each front raised over a basement. On two opposite fronts there are two flights of steps – unlike the Rotonda which has steps on each side. The sequence of rooms is built round a central circular hall which is surmounted by a coffered inner dome, rising just above the level of the roof. Light is admitted through circular windows which are set at the base of the outer dome. Built of lead, the outer dome is constructed to a similar height to that intended by Palladio for the Rotonda (in fact, never built). Smoke from the fireplaces was carried up the dome casing in flues and discharged beneath the cowl of the lantern. Unlike the Rotonda, the windows at Mereworth are without shutters and are of the sash type. Also, the sides of Campbell's porticoes are supported by columns and not arches as in the prototype.

Campbell's other works include Stourhead, Wiltshire (1725), for the London banker Henry Hoare, which in plan and elevation derives from Palladio's Villa Emo at Fanzolo. Here he introduces a

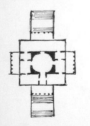

Mereworth Castle, Kent

four-columned portico raised over a rusticated base and rising to roof level. The portico led through an arched entrance to the entrance hall, stair, hall and chapel. Smaller rooms were on either side.

In Norfolk, Campbell managed to secure the patronage of Sir Robert Walpole for Houghton Hall (1722–29) which echoes Palladio's Palazzo Thiene in plan: a rectangular block linked by two quadrants with a kitchen and laundry blocks. The rusticated Venetian windows on the outer bays also echo those of the Palazzo Thiene. These bays were originally to have been surmounted by towers derived from Jones's Wilton House but after Campbell's death domes designed by Gibbs were substituted. The entrance hall is a 40-foot cube in imitation of that by Jones in the Queen's House, Greenwich.

Richard Boyle, third Earl of Burlington, would have been introduced to architecture as one of the 'polite arts' studied as a matter of course by the aristocracy. From an early age he was won over by the architectural message of Palladio and was a subscriber to volume one of *Vitruvius Britannicus* in 1715. In 1719 he revisited Italy on a second 'grand tour', taking with him a copy of the *Quattro Libri*. While in Rome he met William Kent who was there studying painting. A close friendship developed and Kent was brought back to England by Burlington to be installed first in his London home in Piccadilly and later at Chiswick. As Burlington never signed drawings it is hard to determine to what extent any one idea is his own or that of Kent.

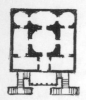

If the overall plan of Chiswick Villa (1725–29) is Burlington's, the interior decoration is Kent's. It is a free interpretation of Palladio's Villa Rotonda, Scamozzi's Villa Pisani at Lonigo and Serlio's design for a villa in Book VII of his treatise of 1575. It is a square block with a Corinthian portico on one side raised only on a rusticated basement. The garden front is adorned by triple Venetian windows. The façade is of plaster scored to simulate stone blocks. Like the Pisani, it has no attic storey but a sloping roof to an octagonal lantern and saucer dome. Each alternate bay of the drum is pierced with a thermal window to admit light to the octagonal hall. Chimneys are cleverly disguised in the form of obelisks.

The disposition of the

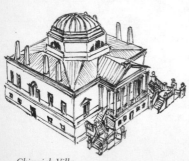

Chiswick Villa

Chiswick Villa: salon. The apsidal coffering is based on that in the Temple of Venus and Rome, in Rome (top)

Chiswick Villa: the octagonal central hall showing coffering and thermal window

rooms round the central hall is similar to the Rotonda
with proportions relating to the cube and circle. On
the garden front the apsidal salon is of double-cube
proportion. The gilt coffering is from Palladio's reconstruction of that in the Temple of Venus and Rome.

Another work which was a joint collaboration
between Burlington and Kent was Holkham Hall
(1734–64), built for Thomas Coke, Earl of Leicester.

Since his return from Italy, Coke had wanted a
larger house in which to display his collection of antiquities and paintings. Campbell and Matthew
Brettingham were consulted but the final design is
strongly influenced by detail from Burlington's
Chiswick Villa, and the plan from his Tottenham Park,

*Holkham Hall,
Norfolk: the south or
garden front*

*Holkham Hall:
entrance hall or
'Egyptian Hall'*

Wiltshire (1722), in which he first used a central-block plan with four linked wings. This in turn derives from Palladio's Villa Mocenigo. Coke wanted Holkham to be a latter-day Roman villa. He even insisted on the use of brick made on the estate and fired to resemble the yellowish brick of the Tiber Valley. The entrance hall was inspired by Palladio's description of an ancient basilica or Egyptian hall based on his interpretation of Vitruvius. It is flanked by colonnades of alabaster Ionic-ordered columns raised on a podium. At the salon end is an apse, the line of columns continued in front like a screen, as in Palladio's S. Giorgio Maggiore. The frieze is derived from the temple of Fortuna Virilis and the coffering from the temple of Jupiter as illustrated by Palladio. As one advances through the hall from the entrance one also notices the continuous lines of antique Greek key and Vitruvian scroll decoration on the podium. While the entrance front is relatively austere, the south or garden front is dominated by a large hexastyle portico.

The influence of the plan and elevation as well as the pyramidal corner towers may be seen in Sanderson Miller's Hagley Hall in Worcestershire (c. 1752), Kent's Horse Guards Building, Whitehall, London (1748–59), and Roger Morris's Lydiard Park, Wiltshire (c. 1740).

Another excursion into the antique by Burlington was his design for the Assembly Rooms at York (1731–32) which, although it had to be fitted into a confined site, was a compromise between the elevation of Palladio's Egyptian hall and an ancient basilica. It is consequently six columns wide and 18 columns deep, with an open floor space proportion of 1:3. This was fine for dancing but the space between the columns and wall was too confined and was subsequently widened in the 1820s.

Externally, many Palladian houses were extremely austere. An example is Lydiard Park where the entrance is through a simple Doric-ordered doorcase. Others, such as Constable Burton Hall, Yorkshire (1768), by John Carr, had a four-columned portico set back from the façade *in antis*. Some have a dignified but subtle elegance which can only be fully appreciated from a distance. Marble Hill House, Twickenham, built for the Countess of Suffolk by Roger Morris and the Earl of Pembroke, was not unlike the earl's London house designed by Colen Campbell, although here there is no portico. Both entrance and garden fronts have a central pediment equal in inclination to the slope of the roof behind. On the centrepiece, the ground or basement storey is rusticated. Above, the *piano nobile* and upper floor

are flanked by giant ordered Ionic pilasters. The bays
on either side are of smooth plaster. The door is set
within a semi-circular arch with an early example of
a fanlight. The pleasing balance of verticality and horizontality is set off on both frontages by a slightly
projected horizontal plat-band between basement and
piano nobile, and banded entablature beneath the
eaves cornice. Two pairs of chimneys rise on either

Marble Hill House,
Twickenham, west
London: 1724–26

side of the pyramidal roof. Roger Morris and the Earl of Pembroke also designed the bridge at Wilton based on unexecuted designs by Palladio. Three others survive, including one at Tsarkoe Selo, near St Petersburg, c. 1776.

Wilton House, Wiltshire: Palladian bridge inspired by Palladio's description of bridges in his Quattro Libri, *his design for stone bridge in Venice and a drawing by Scamozzi for a stone bridge supporting a colonnade of shops*

Palladian taste lasted until the last quarter of the eighteenth century. It was overtaken by the Adam brothers with their new vocabulary of architectural ornament based on a re-interpretation of Roman sources such as Diocletian's palace at Spalato and excavations at Pompeii and Herculaneum, and later by the austerity of the Greek revival. Kedleston Hall near Derby, begun by James Paine and Matthew Brettingham in about 1758 and completed by Robert Adam, may be said to mark the division.

14

The Advent of
Town Planning

There was no example of considered or formal town planning before the 1630s. Many towns consisted of barely more than one main street of narrow-fronted jettied buildings and insanitary side alleys and courts which received little direct sunlight. The most open and impressive area would have been the market place, or a space adjacent to the parish church where the town hall, perhaps over a colonnade, a grammar school linked to the neighbouring parish church, or a trade guild would have been located. Nothing in Britain rivalled the grandeur of a formal continental town centre such as that of Vicenza in Italy, or Paris as it was developed from the reign of Henri IV, or the purpose-built planned grid town of Richelieu. It was the Place Royal (Place des Vosges) (*c.* 1605) which inspired Jones's layout of Covent Garden in the

1630s. The opportunity to rebuild London after the Great Fire to a grid plan by Wren, focusing on St Paul's and the Royal Exchange, had to be abandoned due to cost. However, speculative development of terraces of brick and stucco houses had been introduced at Lincoln's Inn Fields before the fire and this formality was continued in the brick courts and King's Bench Walk of the Inner and Middle Temple. In the first formal squares, such as St James', planned by Lord St Albans in the 1660s, uniformity of façades was not adhered to. A greater attempt to do so was made in the first formal provincial development, that of Queen Square, Bristol (c. 1705).

By 1700 the population of London was growing appreciably and ribbon development was spreading eastwards into the Thames-side hamlets and northwards beyond Piccadilly over land leased by the dukes of Cavendish and Grosvenor. In addition, successive Acts of Parliament began to regulate the use of non-combustible materials for building and there were regulations governing the height and width of façades and new streets. Unfortunately these regulations were not binding on provincial building although disastrous fires such as those in Warwick and Blandford encouraged the rapid adoption of brick in place of half-timbering.

The Advent of Town Planning

The Mayfair and Marylebone district of London's West End was laid out on a semi-grid pattern from about 1720. The street names in themselves convey a feeling for the events and personalities of the period: Hanover Street, Harley Street, Audley Street. These were lined with smart but unpretentious brick terraces for people in the professions, but the open squares were more ostentatious, the height of fashion and the residence of the aristocracy. Although development was speculative and in the hands of a number of landlords, there was an increasing attempt to tie the whole of a terrace or side of a square into one as if it were a palace. This might be emphasised by a plaster-covered centrepiece with pilasters or half pillars and a pediment. Sadly Mayfair has suffered from redevelopment, or sometimes unsympathetic alternatives to the original façades. However, both Georgian Bath and Edinburgh retain a completeness and sense of scale, and so may be studied for typical planning features of the eighteenth and early nineteenth centuries.

In 1700 Bath was small and hardly extended beyond its medieval walls. It had hot mineral springs famed since the Roman era, but barely more than one good inn to accommodate the needs of fashionable visitors. By 1800 it had expanded to cross the Avon into the suburb of Bathwick and climb up the narrow sides of the valley. It also had two assembly rooms (the Pump Room acting for the lower town), an impressive Guildhall with yet another assembly room for balls, the General Hospital or Infirmary for rheumatic diseases, and several hot baths. The late-medieval abbey church was the centre for worship on Sunday mornings before a walk along Grand Parade.

The Georgian creation of Bath was due largely to three personalities: Richard 'Beau' Nash, who arrived in 1705 to be Master of Ceremonies, a post he also held at Tunbridge Wells; Ralph Allen, who arrived in 1715 and who was to own the nearby stone quarries; and John Wood the Elder, who arrived in 1725. Wood had worked for Lord Bingley in Yorkshire and then in London on Grosvenor Square under the builder-architect Edward Shepherd, and on Cavendish Square for the Duke of Chandos. How Wood became involved at Bath is hard to determine for certain. He may have approached one of the Bath landowners, Robert Gay, with plans he had drawn up while in Yorkshire for the speculative development of fields beyond the then city limits. The Duke of Chandos was already proposing development on his own land in Bath.

In 1727 Wood settled in Bath, having taken the risky step of contracting for the building of Queen

ATTIC
STOREY

MODILLIONED
CORNICE

SECOND
FLOOR

PIANO NOBILE
(FIRST FLOOR)

PLAT-BAND

GROUND FLOOR

BASEMENT

WEST END TERMINAL PAVILION   CENTRAL HEXASTYLE PAVILION

Square (1729–36). He probably had the financial support of Ralph Allen who was keen to exploit the virtues of his stone from the Combe Down and Box quarries. Since the development was speculative it was not completed as one project, although the north side was, with a stone terrace directly related to the London squares. Raised on a rusticated basement, the upper floors are flanked by giant ordered Corinthian pilasters. At the centre is a projected pedimented centrepiece of six half columns and at each end there is a projected pavilion of three bays surmounted by an attic storey above the cornice. There

Queen Square, Bath: elevation of north side

is an additional storey in the hipped roof hidden by a parapet. The windows of the main floor or *piano nobile* are topped by alternating triangular and semi-circular pediments.

The ingenuity of Wood as an urban architect and planner can be appreciated when one observes the way in which the terraces climb up Gay Street to the Royal Circus, from the charming bow-fronted house Wood built for himself at the north-east corner of Queen Square and Gay Street. While each house is more or less identical, with a door and two windows on the lower floor, the upper floors have three windows on each. The bow-fronted 21 Gay Street has a fine example of a Venetian window.

The Royal Circus, started in 1754, is Wood the Elder's last and finest work. The buildings surround a circular area of some one hundred metres. They consist of three equal segments so planned that the axis of each of the three approaching thoroughfares is the centre of one of the façades. Like all Bath buildings, they are built over a basement with a light well in front, and the three main floors are dressed with paired columns of the Doric, Ionic and Corinthian orders between each window bay; the roof has yet another floor for domestic staff with dormers hidden behind the oval openings of the parapet. The width of

each house is marked by the tall chimney stacks rising above each party-wall.

The Royal Crescent (1767–75), the work of Wood's son, John the Younger, is linked to the Circus by the unpretentious Brock Street. It is in the form of a great semi-elliptical block comprising 33 town houses overlooking parkland, and was the first of its

Bath: Royal Crescent

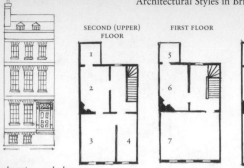

SECOND (UPPER) FLOOR   FIRST FLOOR   GROUND FLOOR

Bath: elevation and plans of typical terrace house
1 powder or dressing room; 2 second bedroom;
3 main bedroom; 4 dressing room; 5 closet;
6 library or study;
7 front drawing room or dining room; 8 closet or kitchen; 9 back parlour;
10 front parlour or dining room; 11 entrance hall

kind in Europe. The masonry is ashlar and the ground or entrance floor serves as a base on which a continuous servis of giant ordered Ionic columns is mounted from end to end. The graceful curve is emphasised by the cornice and balustrade. With its utter rejection of ornament (even window cases), it has the mood of neo-Classicism in which each feature must have a structural function. Only the doors at each side have flanking Doric pillars, entablature and pediment. The mid-point of the curve is emphasised by paired columns and a semi-circular headed window.

This was to be the first of many variations on the circus theme. That at Buxton (*c.* 1780) by John Carr

Buxton, Derbyshire:
The Crescent,
c. 1780

of York has fluted giant Doric ordered pilasters, and with the ground floor in the form of an arcade may derive from the blocks originally surrounding Covent Garden. The Crescent at Clifton (*c.* 1790) is the widest of all. Soon a crescent became an indispensable feature of the fashionable but formal layout of the new spa

Blackheath, London:
The Paragon, c. 1806

towns. Examples include Landsdown Crescent, Cheltenham, and others in the seaside resorts of Brighton and Ramsgate. Even in Bath there were later variations including John Eveleigh's Camden Crescent, employing giant Corinthian ordered pilasters and a rare five-columned centrepiece well off-centre. At Blackheath, south London, the Paragon (*c*. 1806) consists of seven brick buildings each with a slightly concave façade linked by low wings behind a Doric colonnade.

For obvious reasons formal development tended to take place outside the limits of the original settlement. At Cheltenham this stretched outwards on either side of the small medieval town to embrace Landsdown and Pittville. In due course two elegant pump rooms or drinking halls, the Pittville Pump Room (*c*. 1827), with a strongly Grecian flavour, and Montpellier Rotunda (*c*. 1830), with a large coffered dome and lantern derived from John Soane's Bank of England, were built to be the focus of the social scene.

In Edinburgh, shortly to become known as the 'Athens of the North' due as much to its adoption of the Greek revival as the fame of the university, the New Town was to become the largest Georgian urban development in Britain. Between 1767 and 1840 a

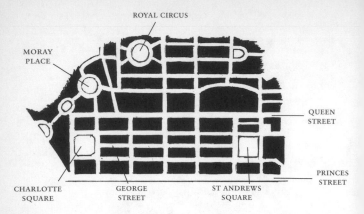

ROYAL CIRCUS

MORAY
PLACE

QUEEN
STREET

CHARLOTTE
SQUARE

GEORGE
STREET

ST ANDREWS
SQUARE

PRINCES
STREET

Edinburgh: plan of New Town

huge area to the north of Prince's Street and sloping down towards the Forth was laid out on a grid plan by James Craig. The principal thoroughfare, George Street, containing the Assembly Rooms, links St Andrew's Square in the east with Charlotte Square in the west. In this overall conception of a New Town built as a complete entity, unlike the piecemeal and speculative way that London's West End had devel-

212

Edinburgh: Charlotte Square, c. 1790, one of the most gracious examples of urban planning in Europe

Cheltenham, Gloucestershire: Montpelier Assembly Rooms, now a bank but with a beautifully restored interior

oped, Edinburgh had more in common with the spacious and monumental grandeur of Nancy or Paris during the reign of Louis XV. During this period a number of celebrated architects, including Sir William Chambers, Robert Adam, Thomas Hamilton and William Playfair, contributed impressive terraces and individual buildings, including assembly rooms and schools in the Greek style such as the Royal High and John Watson's.

As a result of the terrain, Edinburgh's streets

introduce a variety of ground plans which drop down from level to level: Ainsley Place to Moray Place and on to the Royal Circus. Bowed frontages occasionally appear and wrought iron balconies are much in evidence, as they are at Cheltenham. Where but in the Athens of the North could you find an attempt to build a national war memorial in the form of a replica of the Parthenon on Carlton Hill, Edinburgh's own Acropolis?

Nearby Glasgow was not unaffected by the urge

Edinburgh: Royal High School, c. 1825, the Greek Revival at its most austere

for classical grandeur and, although on a very much smaller scale, George Square was completed by 1787.

By the end of the eighteenth century many ports and seaside resorts had terraces, squares and crescents. Even that former medieval port on the River Dee, Chester, witnessed the erection of fine rows of brick terraces and the severe Greek Doric Chester Castle by Thomas Harrison. In nearby Liverpool, which saw the greatest growth of any town in the eighteenth century, elegant brick terraces such as Rodney Street, Canning Street and Abercrombie Square, were laid out. Many had fan lights over doors set into brick arches and flanked by fluted Doric columns. Some have now been restored with sash windows and correctly proportioned glazing bars. The more fashionable houses, such as those in Abercrombie Square, have continuous cast-iron balconies. At the heart of the city the Town Hall (1749–54), by John Wood the Elder of Bath, still stands. The dome was added by James Wyatt (c. 1795), but it remains a magnificent example of the Palladian style.

Another city renowned for its brick Georgian streets and terraces is Dublin – particularly noteworthy are Capel Street and Marriot Square. The stone-built Customs House and Four Courts by James Gandon (1743–1823) overlooking the Liffey owe not

a little to Wren's Greenwich Hospital and even St
Paul's Cathedral.

The British finally discovered the qualities of sea
air in the eighteenth century. Scarborough was the
first so-called resort, followed soon after by Margate,
which popularised the newly invented bathing
machine. Margate's Hawley Square and Cecil Square

*Brighton, Sussex:
Brunswick Square,
c. 1825, grand urban
seaside planning in
stucco over brick*

were in plain undistinguished brick (now much altered). A few miles round the Kent coast is Ramsgate which retains much of its slightly later Regency charm. Here we see brick and white stucco-fronted terraces with the bow-fronted bay and ornamental balcony above. Entrance is up a flight of steps flanked by railings as a protection from the basement well.

It was at Brighton that seaside town planning reached its apogee. If some stucco-fronted terraces might look much like those in Ramsgate or Hastings, few can dismiss the palatial façades of Brunswick Square (c. 1825): bow fronts dressed with giant orders.

Tunbridge Wells, Kent: Calverly Park, 1829–30

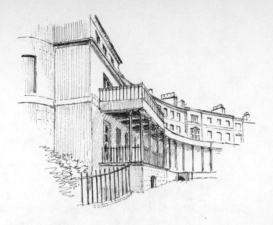

And for those who liked to live in an atmosphere of a planned city state but without the feeling of mass housing by the sea, there were the detached villas by Decimus Burton in Calverley Park, Tunbridge Wells. Built of stone and fronted by cast-iron verandas and long gardens – all that one might desire?

Tunbridge Wells, Kent: Calverly Crescent, 1829–30

15

New Styles and New Materials

Between about 1750 and 1900 the development of British architecture becomes extremely complex, even though the Gothic may seem very much the style of the Victorian era with its wide ranging application from churches to railway stations and public schools to hotels and prisons.

While Walpole was building Strawberry Hill, Chinese style made a brief appearance. The Chinese House at Shugborough, Staffordshire (*c.* 1747), is perhaps the earliest building, followed in 1749 by the Chinese Pavilion at Kew. In 1752 the first five-stage pagoda was built in Shugborough, followed in about 1757 by the more famous version at Kew by William Chambers who published *Designs for Chinese Buildings* in the same year. The Chinese or 'Chinoiserie' went well with the delicacy of the current

OPPOSITE
Glasgow: Caledonian Road Free Church, 1856–57

Rococo interior and is perhaps seen at its finest in the
Chinese Room at Claydon House in Buckinghamshire
(*c.* 1770).

In 1755 the German art historian and archaeol-
ogist Winckelmann published his *Reflections on the
Painting and Sculpture of the Greeks* which led to a
fundamental change in the understanding of classical
history. Winckelmann saw the Greeks as the creators
of classical perfection and the Romans as being
copyists. He felt that the spirit of noble simplicity
and calm grandeur found in their art should be applied

Claydon House,
Buckinghamshire: the
Chinese Room

222

to the art of the present. He further reinforced his views on the supremacy of the Greeks in his *History of the Art of the Ancient World* (1764). His writings fuelled the spirit of the neo-Classical movement which affected architectural development throughout Britain and northern Europe from Paris to St Petersburg, and across the Atlantic to New York and Washington. While in France it was seen as a reaction against the frivolity of the Rococo and the reign of Louis xv, and was to be associated with the moral virtues of the classical world and to be revived by Revolution, in Britain it was more archaeologically based.

Hitherto few British architects had studied in Italy but this now became almost a prerequisite, helped and encouraged by the Royal Academy which taught architecture from its foundation in 1768. The Society of Antiquaries also encouraged the study and examination of classical remains at first hand.

The second half of the eighteenth century is dominated by the work of Robert Adam (1728–92) and Sir William Chambers (1723–96). The two were very different in character: Adam a master of invention and adaptation, with an eye for ornament, and Chambers, cold and aloof and a brilliant draughtsman. The latter continued the late-Palladian tradition as in

Duddingston House near Edinburgh, and Lord Bessborough's villa at Roehampton. In his Somerset House (from 1775), between the Strand and the Thames in London, he produced a work which rises to the grandeur of contemporary building in Paris such as that on the north side of the Place de la Concorde. The Thames frontage is raised on a rusticated terrace pierced with arches reminiscent of those in a Piranesi etching of a prison. The main defect of this façade is the want of a larger dome to create a striking centrepiece.

Robert Adam, born in Scotland, like Chambers spent some time in Italy where he immersed himself in a study of the classical remains. He also crossed the Adriatic to Dalmatia where he made a detailed study of the remains of the Emperor Diocletian's palace at Spolato (Split). He was revolutionary in adapting the vocabulary of ornament found in a Roman domestic building to his own use, although excavations at Herculaneum and Pompeii were beginning to reveal the secrets of the ordinary house and the richness of Roman design and ornament.

Adam believed that the Romans had not been rigid in the use of architectural form and proportion, as revealed at Spolato, and that he was therefore free to adapt their precedent to modern circumstances.

OPPOSITE
Harewood House, near Leeds: the library, a beautiful example of Adam interior decoration

This earned the derision of Chambers, who kept Adam from membership of the Royal Academy.

Adam was a master of adaptation, particularly in a confined space, and a number of his commissions were for the completion or conversion of existing houses, such as Kedleston (*c.* 1761), Syon (*c.* 1763), and Osterley (*c.* 1762). Harewood near Leeds was his first commission and completely his own work. In this and his other great houses we see how he used plaster to magnificent advantage on walls and ceilings. Frequently repeated ornament includes anthemions based on the honeysuckle, arabesques, ribbons, *paterae* or circular flower patterns, candelabra, vases, urns and friezes of linked swags or festoons, or sphinx and putti or repetitive Greek key. Moulded surfaces were often painted white while flat wall and ceiling surfaces were in pastel shades of pink, blue and green. Where he could not use actual marble he used alabaster and scagliolo, a compound of marble fragments, plaster of Paris, glue and paint.

Kedleston Hall, Derbyshire: the south front

At Kedleston the Roman is invoked in the 'Egyptian' entrance hall, hardly less grand than Holkham. Beyond is a circular salon crowned with a coffered dome reminiscent of the Pantheon. The south front is a conscious derivation from the Arch of Constantine. At the other extreme to the spacious grandeur of Harewood and Kedleston are his intimate interiors of 20 St James's Square and 20 Portman Square in London, which combine elegant staircases with rooms of the utmost delicacy.

Adam's Scottish contributions should not be overlooked and include in Edinburgh the University or College, Registry House, and the north side of Charlotte Square. In Old Calton burial ground he built a mausoleum to the philosopher David Hume based on the Mausoleum of Theodoric in Ravenna. In Berwickshire he completed Mellerstain House (*c.* 1768) and converted Culzean Castle to a battlemented exterior with turrets. Adam had a number of less inventive followers including James Wyatt (1746–1813), whose Heaton Hall, Manchester, might pass as a fair imitation.

By the beginning of the nineteenth century the more austere Greek revival was under way in the hands of a number of notable exponents. The revival may be said to have begun with the designing of the

Doric portico for Hagley Hall, Worcestershire (1758), and the Doric temple at Shugborough (*c.* 1760) by James 'Athenian' Stuart. Thomas Hamilton has been mentioned in connection with Edinburgh and in Chester Thomas Harrison's entrance to the Castle is like the contemporary Brandenburg Gate in Berlin, modelled on a reconstruction of the Propylaea (entrance) to the Acropolis in *The Antiquities of Athens* by Stuart and Revett, and Le Roy in France.

Cambridge: Downing College

William Wilkins (1778–1839) who had been a classical scholar at Cambridge before extensive travels in Italy, Greece and Asia Minor, produced several fine essays in the style. His Grange Park, Hampshire (*c.* 1808), is the most perfect adaptation of the Doric temple style to a country house. At Downing College, Cambridge (1806–20), he designed a series of detached stone blocks round three sides of a large court using the Ionic order in the large porticoes.

The most appropriate buildings to be clad in a Greek skin are museums and none more so than the British Museum in London. Founded in 1753 in Montague House it had by the 1820s become too small and so was totally rebuilt by Sir Robert Smirke who fronted it with 48 huge Ionic columns. Karl Friedrich Schinkel clad his Altes Museum, Berlin, in Ionic columns at the same time. As late as 1882 Preston Museum, Lancashire, was built in a severe Ionic manner with an Ionic frontage strongly reminiscent of Schinkel's Schauspielhaus in Berlin. George Basevi (1794–1845) used the Corinthian order to dramatic effect on the Fitzwilliam Museum, Cambridge. In Edinburgh the narrow causeway linking the Mound with Princes Street and the New Town became the site for the Royal Scottish Academy and National Gallery, both in the severe Greek Doric by William Playfair.

Perhaps the most inappropriate usage for the pure Greek temple style is to adapt it to serve as a Christian church. St Pancras Church in London (1819–22), by H W and W Inwood is modelled on the Erechtheum in Athens. The portico is Ionic and side vestries reproduce the famous caryatids, one of which had recently arrived in London by courtesy of Lord Elgin and the Turks. The tower reproduces elements from the Athenian Tower of the Four Winds which was carefully documented in The Antiquities of Athens and which had been reproduced as one of the garden build-

Brighton, Sussex: the Royal Pavilion

ABOVE *Sezincote,*
Gloucestershire
BELOW *Cronkhill,*
Shropshire

*Blaise Hamlet, near
Bristol, Avon*

ings at Shugborough in 1765. In Glasgow, Alexander 'Greek' Thompson built several fine churches in the style. His Caledonian Road Free Church (1856–57) has an Ionic portico set on an enormous podium containing two doors like entries to a treasury. To one side stands a dominating tower.

A current or feeling which swept through both the Greek and Gothic revivals is that of the Romantic Movement. It embraced landscape gardens and urban parks. Perhaps its greatest master was John Nash whose work ranges from the oriental at Brighton inspired by Sezincote, Gloucestershire, through Italianate villas in the Welsh marches and Gothic villas in Devon, the 'cottage *ornée*' at Blaise Hamlet, to urban planning to rival Wren's visions. Nash knew the right people, not least the Prince Regent and had a healthy disregard for money – the cause of his eventual downfall. His greatest work was the layout of Regent's Park and its link through Regent Street to the centre of London. His terraces seen through the autumn leaves of Regent's Park were described by the late John Summerson as 'dream palaces' to rival Wren's Greenwich.

East Cowes Castle, Isle of Wight

233

Conceived as an area of villas and terraces for the professional classes, ranged round a park which was to contain yet another palace, and a national Valhalla, and linked to the West End by a series of broad thoroughfares it was planning on a scale to rival Napoleon's Paris. Although not completed on such a lavish scale, Park Crescent (c. 1812) and Cumberland Terrace (c. 1825), have a sense of theatre about them: the grand sweep of cast iron Ionic columns form a continuous portico to Park Crescent, and the long terraces of austere white stucco with Ionic pavilions and huge ten-columned portico, linked to each other

Regent's Park, London: Chester Terrace

234

by miniature triumphal arches is breath-taking. Only when one goes round the back does one see that the gleaming stucco is a sham, and that they are made of brick.

Apart from the plan of Regent Street, little remains of Nash's original design. The curving Doric colonnade lit by gas was pulled down by the 1850s, and by the end of the century most of the buildings had been replaced by shops and offices. Carlton House Terrace in the Mall still survives however, to mark the southern end of Nash's dream. The basement below the terrace is flanked by cast-iron Doric pillars while the main blocks are of palatial Corinthian.

Something of the legacy of Nash's use of stucco lived on for much of the nineteenth century in the terraces of fashionable Brighton, Hastings, Southsea and Torquay, or his flair for multi-style villas, Gothic or Italianate, in Malvern, Leamington and Harrogate.

Perhaps Britain's most original architect was Sir John Soane (1753–1837), who is best described as a romantic classicist. A Royal Academy medallist, he

Belgrave Road, London: Regency terrace block with Doric portico over entrance

Dulwich College, south London: the Picture Gallery

travelled extensively in Italy and gazed on the ancient Greek temples at Paestum. Appointed Architect to the Bank of England in 1788, he created a vast area of courtyards, colonnades and vaulted and domed chambers behind a wall of Portland stone dressed with Corinthian pilasters, and framed at the corners with temple pavilions from Tivoli. His vaulted halls reduced structure and ornament to its most simple and he virtually created a new grammar of ornament based

on grooves and incised lines of Greek key. He seemed able to reduce classical construction to the simplicity advocated by the French neo-classical theorist, Abbé Laugier. Unfortunately, this ensemble of Piranesian proportion was swept away to be replaced by Sir Edwin Lutyens's buildings in the 1920s. Something of Soane's imaginative use of arches, bare brick surfaces, chambers and overhead lighting does survive in Dulwich College Picture Gallery (c. 1814).

Pall Mall, London: the Reform Club, Charles Barry's interpretation of a sixteenth-century Roman palazzo

*Iron Bridge,
Coalbrookdale,
Shropshire: c. 1779*

A feature of nineteenth-century social and intellectual life was the rise of the club, public library and literary institute. The classical seemed the appropriate style and whilst Decimus Burton (1809–81), felt the Grecian appropriate for the Atheneum complete with a frieze based on the Elgin marbles, a few metres away

in Pall Mall, Sir Charles Barry was building the
Reform Club in the Italianate and based on the
sixteenth-century Palazzo Farnese in Rome.

As Nash was dreaming up his palaces for Regent's
Park and Barry his Italianate contributions to club-
land, so Britain was going through dramatic social

*Liverpool: Albert Dock,
1839–45, brick
warehouses over iron
frame*

change. The population was expanding rapidly and new centres of commerce and industry were springing up. Cast iron, used so effectively on the bridge across the Severn (c. 1779) at Coalbrookdale, was now utilised as the framework and weight-bearing structure of dockside warehouses and the cloth and woollen mills of the north. In London Thomas Telford and Philip Hardwick built St Katherine's Dock in the 1820s: the first enclosed dock warehouse system with floors of London clay brick cladding an iron cage and resting at ground level on immense cast-iron columns. In Liverpool Jesse Hartley, who had trained as a bridge builder in Yorkshire, and who has corresponded with Hardwick over the structure of the St Katherine's warehouses, designed a massive enclosed dock of about 7 acres. Opened by Prince Albert in 1845, the huge brick warehouses rise five storeys above a ground-floor colonnade of massive cast-iron Greek Doric columns broken at intervals by wide elliptical arched bays.

Meanwhile Britain's technological advance was enough to attract the German Romantic architect, Karl Friedrich Schinkel, to make a tour of Britain from Dover to the Menai Straits, from Liverpool to Leith, taking in the warehouses of Manchester and the potteries of Stoke on the way.

16

Gothic Survival
and Revival

In some respects the Gothic style never really died out in Britain, in fact two great examples of this style, the Anglican cathedrals of Guildford and Liverpool, were only completed in 1966 and 1980 respectively. The latter towers over its surroundings with a force and austerity reminiscent of the walls of Albi Cathedral while the Lady Chapel has the flavour of a latter-day Saint Chapelle. As mentioned earlier, Gothic was still the preferred style for much of the seventeenth century in Oxford: University College was rebuilt from *c.* 1634, a hall and chapel at Oriel between 1639 and 1640 and a Gothic chapel at Lincoln College in 1681. Wren added Tom Tower at Christ Church in 1681 and in about 1715 work began on the Codrington quadrangle at All Soul's to the design of Hawksmoor. A close examination of the detail will

Christ Church, Oxford:
Tom Tower, c. 1680,
Wren's completion of
the Tudor quadrangle

give a key to the early eighteenth century approach to the style – it is really Gothic under a classical restraint. For example, the windows are barely pointed and are without tracery. Even a Venetian arch appears between the towers on the east side of the quadrangle.

In London, Hawksmoor designed the two western towers of Westminster Abbey and is attributed with the Gothic tower of St Michael, Cornhill (*c.* 1715). A few miles away on Maze Hill overlooking Greenwich John Vanbrugh built his 'Bastille', a romantic evocation of the Middle Ages continued for the convenience of an eighteenth-century gentleman. Its symmetry and sash windows and the castellated gateposts give it a somewhat toy-like appearance. William Kent, the disciple of Palladianism, also indulged in the 'Gothick'; at Hampton Court he rebuilt the gatehouse of Clock Court with a plaster vault over the passage. He was probably responsible for the rebuilt Shobden church, Hereford and Worcestershire (*c.* 1754), in which we see so well the characteristics of Georgian Gothic. At once the flat coved ceiling proclaims the air of a ballroom turned into a church. The ogee-arched windows look flimsy and the wooden gallery is decorated with large square panels filled with quatrefoils. At the crossing, clus-

Liverpool: the Anglican cathedral, completed in 1980

*Maze Hill, Greenwich:
the Bastille, c. 1717,
Vanbrugh's magnificent
evocation of the
medieval*

tered shafts rise to support a mere plaster arch, when a crossing tower might be expected. Another early Gothick curiosity is the small Banqueting House at Gibside near Durham by Daniel Garrett (*c. 1751*). This has ogee arches, quatrefoils, battlements and sprouting gables.

If there was a revival then Sanderson Miller (1717–80) and Horace Walpole (1717–97) are often seen as the founders. Miller was a Warwickshire gentleman who turned to architecture as a polite archaeological interest. He created sham castles and

Gibside, Tyne and Wear: banqueting house, c. 1751

towers, picturesque cottages and Gothic summer houses, but he is best remembered for the new hall at Lacock Abbey, Wiltshire (1753–55), built for the Talbot family. The exterior betrays its period: windows with flimsy tracery beneath the ubiquitous ogee hood, a rose window in the centre like a star, open tracery on the parapet reduced to the delicacy of lace and the balustrade of the entrance stair pierced with foiled openings.

Horace Walpole was another gentleman of leisure and wealth who turned his mind to architecture and collecting. Son of the prime minister Robert, he is also remembered as having been the greatest correspondent of the period and the author of the first Gothick novel, *The Castle of Otranto*. In 1749 he bought a

Lacock Abbey, Wiltshire, c. 1753–55

cottage at Twickenham and over the next 50 years turned it into one of the greatest attractions for visitors to London. Strawberry Hill grew over each decade as Walpole sent his 'Committee of Gentlemen' out in search of suitable architectural material to reproduce in his expanding house. So the Long Gallery has fan vaulting derived from the Henry VII Chapel, Westminster Abbey, and the Great Parlour and Library derive from illustrations in William Dugdale's *Old St Paul's*. Fireplaces are set in between niched surrounds and beneath canopies: that in the Holbein Chamber is based on the tomb of Archbishop Warham in Canterbury Cathedral while the ceiling is based on that of the 'Queen's Dining Room' in Windsor Castle. By the time the house was complete it had inadver-

Strawberry Hill, Twickenham: Horace Walpole's Gothick villa developed from two cottages into a gentleman's medieval palace between c. 1750–90

Strawberry Hill: the Holbein Chamber

tently introduced a new mood to architectural design which was the keynote of the Picturesque Movement, asymmetry. This was created by the erection of the Round Tower with its stair turreted, forming a junction with the right-angled west wing. Walpole described his house as 'pie-crust Gothick' which will after his death 'be blown away in the wind like dust'. Fortunately it has survived, but not so the greatest extravagance of the revival, Fonthill Abbey, Wiltshire (1795–1812).

Fonthill was the creation of James Wyatt for the eccentric millionaire and author of the oriental tale *Vathek*, William Beckford. At first he wanted a house partly ruined, partly habitable, but was persuaded in favour of the latter. In plan it was basically a cross with an enormous octagonal tower based on Ely Cathedral's octagon. There was a cloister to one side and each wing introduced elements of castellated and collegiate Gothic. Beckford was impatient and hurried Wyatt, resulting in weak foundations. One day the tower collapsed and Fonthill was no more. Its rambling, picturesque asymmetry is left to us in watercolours and engravings after Turner.

By the early nineteenth century Gothic was being used for churches exploiting the new material of cast iron. Appropriately, several of the finest examples are by the man who was the first to analyse the development of the style and place it into a meaningful chronology. He was Thomas Rickman (1776–84), who in 1812 was elected Professor of Architecture at the Liverpool Academy. In 1817 his *An Attempt to Discriminate the Styles of English Architecture from the Conquest to the Reformation* was published and became the cornerstone of the Gothic Revival. He designed a number of churches in Birmingham and the Midlands and several striking examples in Liverpool, his adopted city.

There he struck up a friendship with Thomas Cragg, the proprietor of the Mersey Iron Foundry, who was using cast iron for features in cottages such as fireplaces and door frames. Seeing how cast iron had been used so successfully to span the Severn at

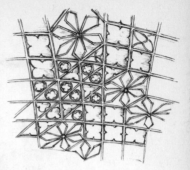

Strawberry Hill: Horace ceiling in the Holbein Chamber

*St John's College,
Cambridge: the 'Bridge
of Sighs', c. 1825*

Coalbrookdale in 1770, Rickman was quick to see the possibility of its application in the construction of churches where space and light were prerequisites. St George's, Everton was his first and although clad completely in stone, has an interior of prefabricated columns, arches, vault ribs, panelling and window tracery. The style is Decorated Gothic. His next work, St Michael-the-Hamlet, completed and opened in 1814, was again in the Decorated style but with a clerestory rarely found before the fifteenth century in parish churches. In St Philip's, Hardman Street (1816), he adopted the Tudor Perpendicular.

However, it was not in Liverpool that Rickman designed his best-known buildings but in Cambridge: New Court and the so-called 'Bridge of Sighs' at St John's College (c. 1825), employing Perpendicular and Tudor. Perhaps it is appropriate that Rickman should have worked at Cambridge for it was here that Gothic was to receive the final accolade of approval with the foundation of the Cambridge Camden Society in 1839 for the study of church architecture and ornament, shortly to be termed ecclesiology.

*Houses of
Parliament: Victoria
Tower, c. 1840–60*

17

Victorian Gothic

At this point in time it is possible to assess and appreciate the Victorian contribution to our architectural heritage objectively. It is also possible to see the change between the antiquarian approach of Walpole and his contemporaries and the scholarly approach based on an archaeological study of the medieval of A W N Pugin and the Victorians.

It was Rickman who in 1817 first put the development of Gothic architecture into a clear stylistic sequence. Shortly afterwards he was commissioned to design the New Court and Bridge of Sighs at St John's, Cambridge. At neighbouring Trinity, the classicist William Wilkins added the New Court, and at King's he built a screen and lodge dividing the Great Court from King's Parade. All of these additions were in the late Perpendicular which in the case of King's fitted perfectly with the dominating chapel. Indeed the Perpendicular style was in fashion among early revivalists; St Luke's Chelsea by James Savage

(1819–25) shows the strong influence of King's College Chapel. The Gothic was also now seen as the style for grammar schools such as King Edward's, Birmingham, designed in the Tudor Perpendicular style by Sir Charles Barry (1795–1860).

The year 1836 marked another turning point in the Gothic movement. Barry won the competition for a design for the new Houses of Parliament to replace those burnt in 1834, and Pugin, who collaborated with Barry in the design but who was officially barred because he was a Roman Catholic, published his *Contrasts*. Here Pugin upheld the virtues of medieval architecture in contrast to the consciousness of the prevalent Renaissance style. As a Catholic convert he believed the building of Catholic churches to be a religious necessity. He also believed that it was not good enough merely to copy form or ornament, but that medieval structural principles had to be studied and revived. Interiors had to conform to the ritualistic needs of a revived faith. In *Contrasts* he asserted the superiority of fourteenth-century Gothic, and in a revised edition of 1841 he illustrated what he saw as the original grandeur of a medieval town, and that at the present 'contaminated' by classicism and industry.

In 1841 Pugin published *The True Principles of Pointed or Christian Architecture* in which he wrote that the Gothic was the only style suitable for a Christian church, and that a successful architect must be a practising Christian. Pugin therefore saw the revival of Gothic as a moral crusade and pursued it with fanatical zeal.

Sadly Pugin is not always credited with a hand in the design of the Houses of Parliament. Whilst the basic plan is Barry's, the detail – including the Clock Tower and Victoria Tower – is Pugin's. He attended to all internal furnishings, even down to the ink wells. At Scarisbrick Hall, Lancashire (1838), he attempted to create a great house to a medieval pattern and introduced a clock tower which has a distinct affinity with that at Westminster.

Although Catholic Emancipation had been granted in 1829, the restoration of the Hierarchy did not come until 1851 and Pugin could not therefore rely solely on Catholic patrons, although Charles Scarisbrick and the sixteenth Earl of Shrewsbury were both Catholic. For the latter he built St Giles, Cheadle, Staffordshire (1841–46), a superb expression of Pugin's veneration of fourteenth century, mid-pointed or Decorated style. Another Catholic commission was for St George's, Southwark (c. 1840), which like Cheadle was to have had a western spire above the tower, but this was never built. Fortunately, the impetus given by the foundation of the Cambridge Camden Society in 1840 with its added emphasis on liturgical requirements gave Pugin the commissions he needed, so in effect this convert to Rome became an ardent disciple of the image of the Victorian Anglican Church. He worked himself to an early death and is buried in his finest church, St Augustine, Ramsgate, Kent.

One of Pugin's ardent disciples was George Gilbert Scott (1811–78), who is said to have designed and restored over 400 churches and 39 cathedrals. Like Pugin, he favoured the fourteenth-century Decorated style, so much so that when commissioned to restore the burnt-out shell of the medieval Perpendicular Doncaster parish church he insisted on rebuilding it in the Decorated style. Perhaps his most famous or familiar building is the Midland Hotel, St Pancras (c. 1868), which was basically a revision of his rejected design for the Foreign Office competition. The Liberal prime minister Lord Palmerston associated the Gothic with High Church Toryism. Of red brick with stone for the hundreds of windows, including the dormers in the steep pitched roofs, the Midland Hotel has a certain north German or Baltic feel about it. From some angles the roof silhouette is one of the most romantically picturesque in London,

London: St Pancras Station, Midland Hotel, c. 1868, a fitting entry to London for passengers in the Railway Age

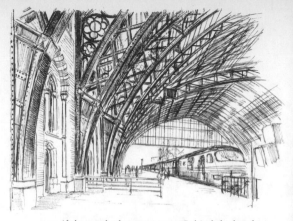

even if the smoke has now gone. Behind the hotel, a magnificent cast-iron roof by the engineer W H Barlow covers the platforms.

Among the other leading revivalists was William Butterfield (1814–1900), who exploited the multi-coloured qualities of brick and stone, so-called 'constructional polychromy'. He came under the influence of the Cambridge Camden Society and its president Alexander J Beresford-Hope, and through him was commissioned to restore St Augustine's Abbey,

St Pancras Station, London: the train shed in which W H Barlow manages to include a Gothic point in the iron work

Canterbury, as a college. By later standards this is reasonably conventional, and the rebuilt Abbots Guest Hall to be used as the library was modelled on the Hall of Mayfield Manor, Sussex.

His All Saints, Margaret Street, Westminster, was built as the model church of the Ecclesiological Society (as the Camden had now become). The interior has a blaze of colour across every wall surface, marble shafts gleam, as do the wrought-iron screen and floor tiles. Decorated the church may be, but its simple forms including window tracery suggest the thirteenth rather than he fourteenth century.

Although a disciple of Pugin, Butterfield was not always prepared to be tied to his rules of taste or design; some felt his polychromatic surfaces distasteful. In academic buildings he introduced a mixture of red brick and creamish stone in horizontal bands and chequer and diamond patterns. His masterpieces in this vein are Keble College, Oxford (*c.* 1870), and Rugby School Chapel.

Butterfield in effect proved that Gothic was a living style capable of fresh interpretation even if architects like Scott felt a debt and duty to the past, as at his Exeter College Chapel which is Sainte Chapelle on a smaller scale. George Edmund Street (1824–81), who trained in Scott's office, was a prolific

London: All Saints,
Margaret Street,
1850–59

*Oxford: Exeter
College Chapel,
c. 1857*

London: the Law Courts in the Strand, c. 1866–83

architect, and as an active member of the Ecclesiological Society was responsible for some outstanding churches. His St James the Less, Pimlico, London (1860), is an excellent example in which he assimilated continental Gothic elements. He was also responsible for some outstanding domestic commissions and the latter part of his life was taken up with the Law Courts (1866–81) in the Strand. Here he was strongly drawn to the French thirteenth century style with lancets, blind arcading and turrets. The stone-vaulted great hall is a masterpiece.

Another revivalist drawn to the French thirteenth century Gothic was John Pearson (1817–97). His earlier works included picturesque small castles and manors such as Treberfydd, Breconshire (1848), but his outstanding work is Truro Cathedral, begun in 1880. It looms over the small city in its golden grey granite. Cruciform in plan, it has a distinct flavour of thirteenth-century Chartres. Only the introduction of a bold crossing tower is untypical since the French had largely abandoned these by the early thirteenth century in cathedrals.

The writer and critic John Ruskin was drawn further afield in his admiration of continental Gothic and his *Stones of Venice* advocated its ornament as appropriate for English building. His words were immediately felt by Thomas Deane and Benjamin Woodward in their University Museum, Oxford (1855), and in the 1870s numerous Venetian Gothic office blocks and even warehouses sprouted throughout Britain's rapidly developing cities.

Alfred Waterhouse (1830–1905) was another

City of London: a Victorian 'Venetian' Gothic office block

Oxford: University Museum, c. 1855. A cathedral of cast iron, ideal for the exhibition of life-size casts of prehistoric animals

outstanding and prolific exponent of the movement. More eclectic in taste due to his extensive European travel, one of his first works was the now demolished Assize Courts, Manchester (1859), in which he used Venetian Gothic. His most memorable building, indeed perhaps the most memorable of the whole Victorian era, is Manchester Town Hall (1867). It stands solid on an irregular site, its main façade dominated by a splendid tower, asserting Manchester's place as the second city of the empire. However, Waterhouse's vision extended back in time to the Romanesque which he had seen, especially in Germany. His finest work in this style is the terracotta-banded Natural History Museum, South Kensington (1873–81). The deeply recessed portal and tall flanking towers suggest a middle Rhineland cathedral. The capital carving on the jamb shafts of the entrance depict a wide variety of animals and plants. More northern German is his striking red brick and tiled Prudential Assurance Building in Holborn (1879).

By the late 1870s the fanatical enthusiasm for Gothic had begun to wane – other periods and styles were creeping in. For example, Gothic was no longer seen as the only style suitable for academic buildings. Near Egham in Surrey, W H Crossland built the most remarkable university building of all, Royal Holloway

Manchester Town Hall, c. 1867: perhaps the grandest of all the grand Victorian Gothic civic halls

City of London: the Prudential Assurance Building in Holborn, c. 1879

College (1879–87), a vast sixteenth-century château in red brick and white stone in the style of the sixteenth-century Loire châteaux of François I. Even at Cambridge, that bastion of ecclesiology, Basil Chapney's classical design for the Divinity School was chosen in preference to the Gothic. At Dulwich College, south London (1866–70), by Charles Barry

Egham, Surrey: Royal Holloway College, c. 1879–87

South London: Dulwich College, 1866–70

junior, a form of Italianate Romanesque intermingled with the influence of the German 'Round Arch' fashion and decorated with terracotta panels, makes its appearance again intermingled with the Gothic. At Marlborough College, Wiltshire, the early eighteenth century Queen Anne style was used to harmonise with the buildings of the town. Even the Egyptian made a brief appearance, as in the Penzance Egyptian House (*c.* 1840), Canterbury Synagogue and Marshall's Mill,

Leeds: Marshall's Mill, c. 1838–40. Egypt comes to industry

Cardiff Castle,
c 1865–70:
William Burges at
his most
extravagant

Leeds (1838–40).

Gothic-style villas and railway stations sprouted throughout Britain, with even baronial Gothic in the Highlands imitating Balmoral. However, if there must be one Gothic revivalist who beats all others in terms of his romantic approach to the Middle Ages, as if his creations were from the background to a Pre-Raphaelite painting or a manuscript of the Duc de Berry, it is William Burges (1827–81). He had the good fortune to come under the patronage of the Marquis of Bute, whose wealth was partly built on Welsh coal and Cardiff docks. As Burges had studied French medieval castles through the *Dictionnaire de l'Architecture Française du XI au XIII siècle* by Viollet-le-Duc he was the ideal architect to turn the remains of the Norman fortification of Cardiff into a latter-day Carnaervon, and more romantic at that. Its walls are tall, machicolated and sprout numerous towers, some with turrets and spires. The interior is ablaze with marble, coloured floor tiles, and wall paintings of Arthurian legend which through complex symbolism demonstrate Burges's great scholarship.

About eight miles north of Cardiff is yet another work by Burges, Castell Coch, set on a wooded hillside like something out of Burgundy, or more appropriately, Camelot. Austere it might appear externally,

Castell Coch, South Glamorgan: c. 1875–81

Edinburgh: nineteenth-century Gothic villa

but inside it is such a riot of colour as to almost convince one that life was better in the Middle Ages. Lady Bute's bedroom is crowned by a dome. Even her wash-stand is flanked by battlemented towers. Such eccentricity is hardly to be rivalled except in the romantic dream world of Ludwig of Bavaria.

In the real world of expanding cities and industrial suburbs, domestic architecture was much more basic and functional, although it was often sufficient

Oxford, Norham Gardens: Victorian Gothic villas for the expanding academic community, c. 1870

to give an immediate social definition to an area. While detached villas might still feature pointed doorways and Gothic turrets, there was a growing preference for Tudor with wide mullioned and transomed windows set into red brick interspersed with chequer-work terracotta tiles, or stone dressings as in some of the best examples in North Oxford, sometimes described as the finest surviving upper-middle-class Victorian suburb.

In such suburbs many houses were semi-detached, however at the other extreme there were the miles and miles of two-up, two-down working class streets lined

Loughborough, Leicestershire: late Victorian corner-of-terrace shop. Brick patternwork over the windows adds character

Canterbury, Kent: Victorian terraces TOP *typical two-up, two-down* BELOW *suburban housing*

with flat fronted terraces without a bath or indoor toilet. The only visual break would come at the end of a street with a corner shop, or public house which might offer a little decorative relief. All this might seem remote from the visions of Pugin and Ruskin, and the colourful ritualistic world of the ecclesiologists.

London, Shaftesbury Avenue: late Victorian-early Edwardian public house

*Firth of Forth: the Forth
Bridge, 1883–90*

18

From the Forth Bridge to Canary Wharf and Beyond: the Twentieth Century

By the last decade of the nineteenth century architecture had moved into the realm of engineering and a lively debate started as to the aesthetics of what some saw as the products of the machine age. In 1777–79 Abraham Darby had spanned the Severn with his magnificent cast-iron arched bridge which was seen as having an 'acquired beauty'. However, where was this to be seen in the Forth Bridge, built between 1883 and 1890?

Designed by Sir John Fowler and Sir Benjamin Baker, it consists of three huge cantilevered towers linked by side spans to each other and to approach viaducts on each side of the Forth which was at its narrowest point but too deep to be bridged by a conventional viaduct. In any case the North British

Railway Company could not risk another Tay Bridge disaster. It was built of steel which, unlike iron, would expand and contract under pressure rather than snap. Fowler and Baker applied the laws of physics to the structure. For instance, to allow for the vibration of passing trains, the linking sections of the central cantilever are laid against, but not fixed to, the outer cantilevers. This also applies to the track sections from the outer cantilevers to the approach viaducts. Allowance was also made for the fact that the east side would warm up in the morning sun and the west in the afternoon, so producing continuous expansion and contraction of the girders and tubular steel towers. Since its opening in 1890 the Forth Bridge has earned a place in the affection of the British nation even if it does keep open the debate as to whether it is architecture or engineering, or both.

Just four years later in 1894 Tower Bridge was opened across the Thames: two cast-iron towers clad in an elaborate stone skin of Gothic detail. In the centre two huge bascules rise to allow the passage of ships.

By the end of the century architecture had become a fully chartered profession. Although still taught at the Royal Academy, it was now joined by courses at Regent Street Polytechnic and a college at Liverpool incorporated into the university in about 1895. The

Royal Institute of British Architects was founded in 1834. The system of architectural apprenticeship or pupillage continued although increasingly a formal prescribed academic training became the norm of future designers. The profession was given a further label of distinction by the magazine *The Builder,* founded in 1842, and by the end-of-the-century *Architectural Review.*

It was the lift developed by Elisha G Otis in New York in the 1850s which really transformed the size of buildings, not only in the United States with the steel-framed skyscrapers of New York and Chicago, but the hotels, stores and office blocks of the British cities. The Baroque seemed to exude the right quality of confidence for Britain as she sailed into the iron-clad era immediately before the First World War. It was a mixture of Wren and Vanbrugh embellished with a flavour of Garnier's Paris Opera. The flourish of the Baroque was particularly applicable to the new theatres and music halls which certainly in their interiors tried to capture a little of contemporary Paris and Vienna.

Of civic buildings, Cardiff City Hall and Law Courts by H Lanchester and Edwin Richards attempted to celebrate Cardiff's rise as the most important coal-exporting port of the empire. Another work of theirs is Deptford Town Hall, London, which although much smaller celebrates the borough's naval connection with statues of naval heroes set into canopied niches. Other notable London Baroque town halls include nearby Woolwich and Lambeth, the latter with a tower which looks distinctly Wren and Borromini. There was also a vogue for domes at this time, most notably on the Wesleyan Central Hall, Westminster (1905–11). While the outer dome is of lead, the inner over the central hall is of reinforced concrete developed in France by Auguste Perret. That on the Old Bailey (1900–06) echoes, perhaps rightly, the architecture of Wren. At Stockport, Cheshire, the town hall is covered by a dome. On the south bank of the Thames, almost opposite Barry and Pugin's Gothic Houses of Parliament, County Hall by Ralph Knott arose between about 1905 and 1922 with a breath-taking central concavity of Bernini proportions. An additional strength or ruggedness is given by the arched bays of rusticated stonework. The fashion for heavy rusticated stonework is also seen on the head-quarters of Norwich Union Insurance in Norwich by C J Skipper. Numerous other town centres up and down the land have their corners of Baroque grandeur.

With the electric lift, stores and hotels rapidly increased in size. The steel frame was used for the basic structure and clad in stone or brick. The large shop or store was really a Parisian invention of the late nineteenth century with the Bon Marché of 1876 and Printemps, c. 1880. In England the Marshall and Snelgrove shop in Oxford Street, London, by Octavius Hansard (c. 1876) was the earliest. By 1900 they were rising fast: Harrod's in Brompton Road in Baroque yellow terracotta tiles (c. 1897–1905) still exudes Edwardian opulence, Selfridges in Oxford Street (1910), is in the High Renaissance style with giant ordered half pillars of white stone.

Hotels were built to cater for the increasing tourism encouraged by a developed railway system, although there were clear social divisions between those who stayed in cheap seaside lodgings and those who stayed at a resort, spa or city according to the recommendation of Murray's, Baedeker or other guidebooks. For the latter the grand hotel was born and the Grand Hotel, Scarborough (1863–67) was one of the first, conveying a distinct flavour of the French Second Empire style of Napoleon III. The Grosvenor Hotel, London, adjacent to Grosvenor Place, is another major example in this style.

By the early years of the twentieth century ostentation tended to be increasingly reserved for interiors. A formal classicism strengthened in its weight by rusti-

London: Selfridges, c. 1910, the perfect classical department store, stone over a metal frame

cated courses prevailed in some of the major London
hotels. Norman Shaw's Piccadilly Hotel (1905–08)
has a ground colonnade filled by shops, while above,
two pavilions are linked by a long free-standing Ionic
colonnade. The Ritz Hotel, again in Piccadilly, by

*London: the Piccadilly
Hotel, 1905–08*

287

Charles Mewès and Arthur Davis (1903–06), also has a ground-floor arcade. Above, the windows are divided by vertical rusticated strips and the main floors are divided from the attic stages and roof by an unbroken cornice.

London, Piccadilly: the Ritz Hotel, c. 1905

Although Britain was not to be effected by the Art

Nouveau Movement to the extent of the continent (for example the Barcelona of Gaudí or Brussels of Horta) there was one major British exponent – Charles Rennie Mackintosh – whose greatest work is the Glasgow School of Art. Set on a steep slope, it is angular and restrained in its use of curves; the walls are of granite, and the main link with the continent is the curving ironwork and ornamental projections from the windows. For curve and flow and use of coloured tiles,

Glasgow School of Art,
c. 1897

289

Tukey Café, Leicester,
c. 1900

the quintessential elements of the style, the entrance to the former Turkey Café in Leicester designed by Arthur Wakerley (1900–01) is an excellent example.

The Victorian age had witnessed the transformation of Britain from a land of country to town dwellers. The population settled where industry developed with all the resulting social consequences. Few thought of the health of the people growing up and living under a constant pall of smoke. Sir Titus Salt was an exception in the 1850s, with his model town of Saltaire near Bradford. Here he built homes for his employees, a hospital, chapel, high school and a school of art. This was followed towards the end of the century by Lord Lever's Port Sunlight near Liverpool. Here we find Tudor-style terraces inspired by Cheshire's half-timbered houses, fronted by lawns and tree-lined streets. At its heart stands an art gallery providing cultural refreshment and renewal for those lucky enough to live there. George Cadbury set up a similar but less ambitious development at Bourneville, Birmingham. Out of this was born the Garden City Association, inspired by Ebenezer Howard's *Garden Cities of Tomorrow* (1902).

Howard's ideas differed from Lever's in that a town would not be for one specific industry or firm but created around a number of industries. Each would be a fully contained unit complete with educational and medical facilities as well as shops. It would also have a generous provision of parks surrounded by a protected or 'green' belt of open country. They would be linked by a reliable system of rail communications. The first of these new towns, Letchworth, Hertfordshire, was begun in 1903, and in 1907 land was acquired near Golders Green. Over the next decade Hampstead Garden Suburb was laid out to the design of Sir Edwin Lutyens. The third was Welwyn Garden City, in 1919. The style used was a vernacular country-cottage type with prominent gabled wings. This country vernacular is also to be found in the Well Hall estate, Eltham, built between 1915 and 1917 for the workers of nearby Woolwich Arsenal, although it lacked most facilities, including a public house.

After the First World War further radical changes affected the growth of towns and the ordinary domestic house. The widespread employment of women and girls in the hitherto male-dominated professions and trades led to two or more wage earners in the family and higher social aspirations. Now those who could wanted to leave the inner suburban terraced streets and live in the fresh air of the outer suburbs. So the semi-detached, three- and four-bedroomed Tudor-style brick house was born on a

slightly less grand scale than the prototypes, the middle-class mansions of Bedford Park by Norman Shaw. And so out sped the southern 'electric' trains to Sidcup, or the Metropolitan to Harrow and Pinner, or the Mersey electric railway to Southport. Villages joined towns and towns built by-passes to encourage the motorist to stay outside. Notable is the Kingston by-pass (*c.* 1930) and the Oxford northern by-pass (*c.* 1938), trying at the same time to hold the advance of the semis in check.

The First World War also marked the end of major

Canterbury, Kent: mock-Tudor semi-detached houses, c. 1930

Orchards, near
Guildford, Surrey:
c. 1907

country house building in Britain, partly due to size, cost of upkeep, and the drifting away from domestic employment of those who had been traditionally 'below stairs' for generations. Norman Shaw (1831–1912) had been one of the finest exponents of the art of building for those who desired a 'new' seventeenth or eighteenth century seat. His Smeaton Manor, Yorkshire, for example, has the feel of a Restoration house, while at Bryanston in Dorset he built a Queen Anne styled mansion for the Duke of Portland.

Sir Edwin Lutyens (1869–1944) is usually seen as the last of Britain's traditional architects who could merge the simply practical with a sense of the picturesque. He could design in the Surrey vernacular with steep-pitch brick gables and tall chimneys spreading round a cloistered court as at 'Orchards' near Guildford (1907), or Munstead Wood (1896). He was a master of spatial design comparable to Robert Adam. He liked to exploit local materials whether it be soft clunch stone as at Marsh Court, Hampshire (1901), in which he invokes the Elizabethan style, the Deanery, Sonning, Berkshire, exploiting the warm brickwork of the Thames Valley, or granite at Castle Drogo, Devon (1910–30). At Heathcote, near Ilkeley, he uses classical symmetry to reinforce his use of the Doric order on the ground

Marsh Court,
Hampshire, c. 1901

The Twentieth Century

floor. At nearby Gledstone Hall he pays homage to
Palladio. This very personal use of classicism can be
seen on a grand scale in his work at New Delhi where
he designed the Viceroy's House. Unfortunately,
Lutyens's great plan for Liverpool Roman Catholic
Cathedral got no further than the cavernous crypt.
The Second World War intervened and there was not
enough money to build what would have rivalled
Wren's St Paul's with an even taller dome set over a
massive body of pinkish brick interspersed with bands
of granite. The west front was to be pierced by a huge
central arch harking back to that on the Norman front

Ilkley, Yorkshire:
Heathcote, c. 1930

297

of Lincoln, but also invoking the power of a classical triumphal arch.

If the first two decades or so of the twentieth century seem to continue the process of stylistic revivals, the International Modern Movement began to make an impact in the 1930s, helped by the influx of architects and scholars seeking refuge from the rise of Nazism and Communism on the continent. The first building to show the characteristic plain white

The Deanery, Sonning, Berkshire: 1901

Roman Catholic
Cathedral, Liverpool
(unrealised project):
c. 1930

surfaces, windows set in steel frames and a flat roof was New Ways, Northampton (1925), by the German architect, Peter Behrens. Right angles rather than curves now seem to predominate, a feature of cubism. In 1929 the first British-designed house in the International style suddenly 'sprouted' on a hill above Amersham, 'High and Over' by Bernard Ashmole and Amyas Connell.

The writings of Le Corbusier, first published in English in 1927, were also claiming serious attention. If he could suggest replacing the centre of Paris with 18 immense skyscrapers, was this not the answer to the population problem in British cities as well?

Northampton: New Ways, 1925

Providing the foundations were secure they could stand on thin pilotis (pillars) and rise hundreds of feet into the sky. The first block constructed on this principle in Britain was High Point 1, Highgate, which has all the ingredients of the cubist vision of clean lines, floors of steel-framed studio windows and projected

Highgate, London:
High Point 1, 1930

balconies. While High Point was rising, elsewhere in London the London County Council was engaged in large-scale slum clearance and in their place commissioning wholesale brick flats with endless balconies, looking inward on to courtyards. All now had internal stairways unlike their predecessors of the 1880s, the Peabody Trust tenements. At Quarry Hill, Leeds, flats were built as a conscious attempt to copy a working-class estate in Vienna.

Other foreign architects who worked here

Bermondsey, London: London County Council flats

included the German refugees Erich Mendelsohn and
Walter Gropius, leading figures of the Bauhaus closed
by the Nazis in 1933. Mendelsohn designed the De La
Warr Pavilion at Bexhill (1935–37), in which he intro-
duced a semi-circular glazed stair tower with similar
features to those in his Einstein Tower at Potsdam.
Gropius collaborated with Maxwell Fry on the
Impingham Village College, near Cambridge
(1935–37) – the inspiration of much post-Second
World War school building. Unfortunately the style

Bexhill-on-Sea, Sussex:
De La Warr Pavilion,
1935–37

was largely limited to the southern counties where several hospitals also came under the influence of the International Movement. An excellent example is the Kent and Canterbury (*c.* 1935–37). Its emphasis on long corridors and wards with large steel-framed windows is far removed from the heaviness and gloom of a Victorian infirmary.

A revolutionary industrial building of the decade is Sir Owen Williams' Boots pharmaceutical factory at Beeston, Nottingham (1930–32), which comprises a number of glass-clad bays of reinforced concrete, cantilevered out over a despatch bay running the length of the frontage.

A glass-clad façade which echoes the elegant curve of the superstructure of contemporary Atlantic liners is that of the Peter Jones Department Store, Sloane Square, London, by William Crabtree (1936–39). It six floors form a continuous sequence of rectangular panels along the two entrance façades.

Kent and Canterbury Hospital, c. 1935–37

It became a model for many post-war department stores.

In a small way, the modernisation of the railways and the expansion of the underground system in the London suburbs saw the use of modern materials and design. Some stations, such as Derby, were rebuilt with platform roofing of concrete and glass. Concrete also featured in the roofing for London's underground

Beeston, Nottingham:
Boots factory,
c. 1930–32

*Sloane Square, London:
Peter Jones department
store, c. 1936–39*

station platforms such as those on the Central and
Northern Line extensions. Arnos Grove (1932) has a
huge circular booking hall of brick lit by large steel-
framed windows, part of a programme of modern
station building on London's Underground system
under the inspired guidance of Sir Charles Holden. In

Berlin, Feuerbachstrasse Station (1932) on the then newly-electrified suburban railway has a remarkably similar circular booking hall.

The Second World War really held up architectural progress until the 1950s. In 1951 the Festival of Britain exploited the use of new materials such as aluminium featured in the Dome of Discovery and the remarkably futuristic Skylon, but there was much to be rebuilt or replaced as a result of war without such adventures into the realms of avant-garde design. Mass housing such as the Roehampton Estate (1955) saw the LCC trying to bring the benefits of a green envi-

London: Arnos Grove
underground station,
1934

307

ronment to the urban population. At the same time plans were afoot for the creation of satellite towns outside the large conurbations – Crawley, Harlow, Basildon and Kirby, and in the 1970s Milton Keynes and Peterlee. New airports were developed such as Heathrow and Gatwick with huge terminal buildings spanned by roofs of reinforced steel, long walkways and balconies of concrete.

The Festival of Britain, like the Paris International Exhibition of 1889, left one permanent and well-known building, the Royal Festival Hall by Robert Matthew and Sir Leslie Martin. The exterior was remodelled but the interior introduced a magnificent spatial flow of galleries, landings and open-area restaurants with linking stairways. The ceiling above is supported by slender steel stanchions embedded in concrete.

A few years after the creation of the Festival Hall came the controversial rebuilding of Coventry Cathedral in a modern style which exploited the beauty of bare brick as well as modern stained glass. Designed by Sir Basil Spence, the walls are staggered with alternating bays of brick and windows from floor to ceiling. The glass is by John Piper and Patrick Reyntiens. Few can deny that the sun shining through the coloured glass in dappled patches across the

Bethlehem font and floor is a memorable sight. In the 1960s Liverpool Roman Catholic Cathedral was finally finished over Lutyens's crypt. Designed by Frederick Gibberd, it is circular in plan, the altar set centrally beneath a huge glass lantern.

In the field of higher education there have been some impressive as well as controversial developments. One of the first post-war universities was that of Sussex, begun in 1960 by Sir Basil Spence with a

London: Royal Festival Hall, 1951

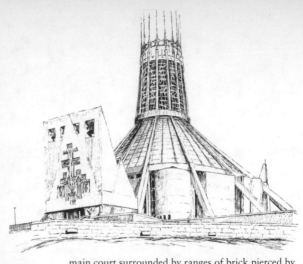

*Liverpool: Roman
Catholic Cathedral,
c. 1960–67*

main court surrounded by ranges of brick pierced by
large windows over arched galleries of concrete and
linking bridges. In all establishments of higher education the emphasis has been increasingly on light, with
wall-to-wall windows. Even if some students have
concrete balconies, the overall effect of some universities and colleges has been rather reminiscent of

prisons with vast areas of bare brick. There have, however, been some notable additions in the university sector such as the Cripps Building at St John's College, Cambridge, (c. 1970) and the Garden Quadrangle at St John's Oxford (c. 1993), with a charming raised terrace garden divided by geometrical white stone beds of plants.

It is in the realm of post-war housing that we find

Falmer: University of
Sussex, c. 1960

*Cambridge: St John's
College, Cripps
Building, c. 1970*

the most controversy. By the late 1950s the prefab was almost a thing of the past as cities and town centres were to undergo 'comprehensive redevelopment' which, in some cases, swept away what the bombing had left. In their place, large areas were transformed into inhuman 'concrete jungles', such as Birmingham's Bullring. What was not designated for urban motorway was given over to high-rise flats reaching ever-increasing heights as the decades passed. These were not luxury constructions like High Point but often built on the cheap of inferior materials, with

Oxford: St John's College, Garden Quadrangle, c. 1993

313

insufficient protection against damp. The collapse of
Ronan Point, east London, in 1968 marked the
turning point in high-rise thinking. Few had an infra-
structure such as shops; when lifts broke down or were
vandalised, the occupants were trapped. Now the aim
is to return to low-rise terracing so that a sense of
community, such an essential part of daily life, can be
re-established.

In 1960 London witnessed the building of the
giant headquarters of Shell Petroleum – the age of the
skyscraper office block had begun. Two years later the
Vickers Building on Millbank was the first structure
to exceed the height of St Paul's. Unlike the Shell
offices, simply a rectangular block of steel clad in
stone, the Vickers Building is largely glazed and angled

*Blackheath, south
London: open-plan low-
rise terrace housing,
c. 1970*

314

*London: Centrepoint,
c. 1960, with the tower
of St Giles in the Fields,
c. 1730, a perfect
contrast of styles*

London: LEFT *the Post Office Tower, c. 1964* RIGHT *Lloyd's of London, c. 1978–86*

to reflect the sun. Between 1962 and 1965 Centrepoint by Richard Seifert arose at the junction of Oxford Street and Charing Cross Road. Although provoking controversy, it has a subtle curve and ripple effect created by the concrete divisions of each floor. Built at the same time, the nearby Post Office Tower, a slender cylinder of steel and glass, proved that technology could be beautiful.

Can this be said of Richard Rogers's Lloyd's Insurance tower in the City of London (1978–86)? It is a huge glass cavern with a semi-circular roof like Paxton's Crystal Palace. The structure is covered by stainless-steel cladding which is fully exposed to view

London, Canary Wharf: model of the entire scheme, c. 1985

inside, along with the ducting and piping and lift casing on the outside. It is altogether a more successful work than Rogers' earlier Pompidou Centre, Paris, and looks highly effective in blue floodlighting.

In terms of size, Canary Wharf in London's Docklands outstrips anything in the City of London; No.1 Canada Square tower is currently the highest office building in Europe. So far only half the scheme has been completed and the tower stands supreme. Designed by Cesar Pelli, it rises almost sheer to its pyramid roof. In some respects it is reproduction of the Pelli towers seen in several American locations including Manhattan.

By the late 1980s the terminal railway station was seen as a piece of architecture which could be hidden from view, after all with electricity having replaced steam traction there was no need for the huge cast-iron roofs above the platforms. The space could be used instead for offices. Certainly, after the spaciousness of the steam-age station, the enclosed replacement such as that at Charing Cross by Terry Farrell (1987–90), can feel claustrophobic. However, from the outer ends of the platforms it looks an imaginative way of incorporating office floors between the tracks and a curving roof, even if the front seems, when floodlit, like a Broadway stage backdrop. It is beauti-

London: Charing Cross
Station, 1987–90

fully tied together with horizontal and diagonal rods of steel, and supported above the platforms on stout fluted Doric columns.

If the ghosts of the Victorian station builders are writhing at the transformation of Charing Cross and Liverpool Street, of Cannon Street and Euston, they would surely enjoy Nicholas Grimshaw's Waterloo International Terminal (1991–93). Here, a continuous roof of glass, supported on a procession of steel arches, gracefully curves to the plan of the platforms below. The feeling of lightness is in keeping with this new age of high-speed travel.

During the course of the millennium, buildings have changed in purpose and in the materials used in construction. In the Middle Ages, castles were of stone and with the minimum of window space

London: Waterloo International Terminal, 1991–93

afforded to the outer walls. Churches and cathedrals, normally substantially of stone, gradually increased window space as the understanding and use of buttresses spread. It was, however, the nineteenth century that witnessed major technological advance with the introduction of cast-iron girders for load-bearing structures and for piers, as in the cloth and woollen mills of the north. As glass production improved, so cast-iron ribs could be combined with sheets of glass to cover the great roofs of Victorian railway stations: Newcastle, Liverpool Lime Street, Paddington and St Pancras in London.

This century has seen even greater lightness of construction with steel bars and rods creating skeletons clad with skins of stone, brick, concrete, or new materials such as aluminium and sheet plastic. British architecture between the wars owed much to the Bauhaus and the International Movement, and the political events that drove some of the key exponents of these movements to this country. Against this, some see Lutyens fighting a rearguard action to preserve the spirit of Georgian classicism. British architecture since the Second World War has been both confused and exciting.

Dreadful mistakes have been made – perhaps inevitably given the need for rapid rebuilding of war-

London: the British Library by Sir Colin St John Wilson and Leslie Martin, opened 1998

damaged cities. The so-called comprehensive redevelopment zones of Liverpool, Birmingham and Newcastle required the demolition of what remained of Georgian and Victorian streets, to be replaced by architecture emphasising raw concrete. And so a new visual brutalism was born. Stone mellows with age, but concrete simply stains and cracks to expose the reinforcing steel within. The experience of London's South Bank complex in the rain is not particularly pleasant; the same is true of some of the university campuses built in the 1960s. But the mood has changed, and the emphasis now, and where appropriate, is on lightness and colour.

My selection of buildings to mark the millennium makes a positive statement of architectural achievement. The new British Library has to be large and secure but its broad brick surfaces, appropriately broken at intervals, and the sunken entrance piazza of patterned tiles are welcoming. Security is also paramount at the Ruskin Library in Lancaster, yet the result is refreshing and appealing with its sparkling

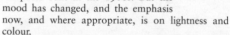

Lancaster University: the Ruskin Library by MacCormac, Jamieson, Prichard, 1998

glazed concrete bands on shell-like walls. The curved surfaces and tall strips of glazing at each end provide a welcome, absent in many other university buildings.

The new Scottish Museum is also, of necessity, solid, but its colour and visual authority are impressive. Indeed, its very outward solidity masks the inner space and transparency created by overhead and high wall glazing. Its external wall surfaces have subtle patterns of coursing which exploit the colour and texture of the Clashach sandstone.

Edinburgh: Museum of Scotland by Benson and Forsyth, 1999

If there is an attraction in the shape and colour

324

of a Roman glass vessel, so there is in several recent glass-clad buildings. The Roy Castle International Lung Cancer Research Centre in Liverpool soars gracefully to a tower at one end. Roughly oval in plan, its curved lines recall the sides of a ship's hull closing to the aluminium prow. The curving roof recalls the deck of a ship as its weight is taken by the aluminium strips below. Fittingly, the National Glass Museum in Sunderland exploits its subject at every opportunity within a reinforced cage of steel. Even the roof has become a transparent viewing platform. For once, we are invited to view the mysterious process of glass production, a far remove from the Victorian idea of the solid factory set behind a high wall – the unwelcoming satanic mill.

Liverpool: Roy Castle International Lung Cancer Research Centre by Franklin Stafford Partners, 1997

If colour is a keynote of late-twentieth-century architecture, then the Glasgow Conference Centre is a stunning addition to the city. Known as the 'armadillo', it exhibits stunning surfaces of gleaming aluminium as the roof curves to become the sides of

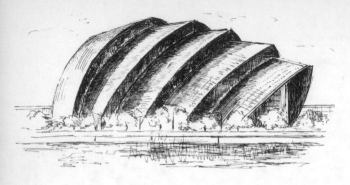

the structure, with its texture amplifying the shimmering sunlight. It is sometimes seen as Scotland's answer to the Sydney Opera House.

The Millennium Dome may be seen as a building opening outwards rather than in, exploiting tensioned steel wire holding a taut surface of fabric panels. From a distance it almost seems to hover, as if a giant spaceship were landing on the tip of the Blackwall peninsula. The structure of diagonal tension cables and twelve yellow pylons makes an interesting contrast with the nearby late-Victorian gasholder; the widest

Glasgow: Scottish Exhibition and Conference Centre, by Norman Foster and Partners 1997

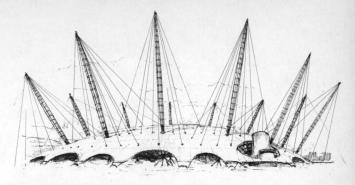

dome and the once-fullest gasholder, where design, technology and artistry come together.

Surely these buildings demonstrate that British architecture is alive and vibrant – though still fraught with controversy as the neo-Modernists, technologists, traditionalists and environmentalists continue to fight it out.

Greenwich, London:
Millennium Dome by
Richard Rogers
Partnership and Buro
Happold, 2000

Further Reading

In recent years there have been a number of excellent books on British architecture ranging from informative, non-technical histories aimed at intelligent non-specialists, to lavishly illustrated volumes on specific architects, styles or periods based on the latest research. Photographs and diagrams are increasingly linked to text as expected, as a study of architecture is that of one of the visual arts.

For those seeking specialist text but generous and high-quality illustrations, the volumes of the Royal Commission on Historic Monuments published by HMSO are outstanding. The earliest ones published in the 1920s and 1930s survey buildings up to 1715, but recent volumes include the nineteenth century. The volumes on London (5), and Oxford, Cambridge (2) are out of print, but may be consulted in good reference libraries. More recent volumes include Salisbury Close, Stamford, York, and Kent, Medieval Houses.

The volumes of the Buildings of England series are admirable and indispensable for the study of the architectural heritage of a specific county. Started by the late Nikolaus Pevsner in the 1950s, most have been substantially revised. Similar volumes have been published on Wales, Edinburgh and Glasgow, and Ireland.

GENERAL

B Bailey, *Almshouses*, 1988

M Binney, *Town Houses: Evolution and Innovation in 800 Years of Urban Domestic Architecture*, 1998

R W Brunskill, *Illustrated Handbook of Vernacular Architecture*, 1978

R W Brunskill, *Traditional Buildings of Britain*, 1992

R W Brunskill, *Brick Building in Britain*, 1990

R W Brunskill, *Houses and Cottages of Britain*, 1997

J Chambers, *The English House*, 1985

A Clifton Taylor, *The Pattern of English Building*, 1972

C Clifton-Mogg, *The Neo Classical Source Book*, 1991

H Colvin, *A Biographical Dictionary of British Architects 1600–1840*, 1975

H Colvin, *Architecture and the After Life*, 1991

O Cook, *The English Country House*, 1974

G Darley, *Built in Britain*, 1985

J G Dunbar, *The Historic Architecture of Scotland*, 1968

A Fenton and B Walker, *The Rural Architecture of Scotland*, 1981

M Girouard, *Life in the English Country House*, 1978

M Girouard, *The English Town*, 1990

M Girouard, *Town and Country*, 1992

I Gow and A Rowan, *Scottish Country Houses 1600–1914*, 1995

J B Hilling, *The Historic Architecture of Wales*, 1977

D Lloyd, *The Making of English Towns*, 1984

N Lloyd, *A History of the English House*, 1931 (reprinted 1975)

T Mowl and B Earnshaw, *Trumpet at a Distant Gate: The Lodge as a Prelude to the Country House*, 1985

A Rowan, *Garden Buildings*, 1968

D Watkin, *English Architecture – A Concise History*, 1979

D Yarwood, *The Architecture of England*, 1963

Further Reading

MEDIEVAL

G H Cook, *The English Medieval Parish Church*, 1954
M Hurlimann, *English Cathedrals*, 1961
C Platt, *The English Medieval Town*, 1976
C Platt, *The Architecture of Medieval Britain*, 1990
E Smith and O Cook, *British Churches*, 1964
W Swann, *The Gothic Cathedral*, 1969
G Webb, *Architecture in Britain: The Middle Ages*, 1956
M Wood, *The English Medieval House*, 1965

SIXTEENTH TO EIGHTEENTH CENTURIES

M Airs, *Tudor and Jacobean*, 1982
M Airs, *The Tudor and Jacobean Country House*, 1996
J Bold, *Wilton House and English Palladianism*, 1988
S Bradley and N Pevsner, *London: The City Churches*, 1998
G Cobb, *The Old Churches of London*, 1942
D Cruickshank, *A Guide to the Georgian Buildings of Britain and Ireland*, 1983
D Cruickshank and N Burton, *Life in the Georgian City*, 1990
J S Curl, *Georgian Architecture*, 1993
K Downes, *English Baroque Architecture*, 1966
K Downes, *Hawksmoor*, 1969
K Downes, *Vanbrugh*, 1977
K Downes, *Wren*, 1984
K Downes, *Sir Christopher Wren: The Design of St Paul's Cathedral*, 1988
J Harris, *The Palladians*, 1981
J Harris, *The Palladian Revival: Lord Burlington*, 1994
C Hussey, *English Country Houses: Country Life* (1. Early Georgian; 2. Mid Georgian; 3. Late Georgian), 1955–58
P Jeffery, *The City Churches of Sir Christopher Wren*, 1996
J Lees-Milne, *Tudor Architecture*, 1951

J Lees-Milne, *The Age of Inigo Jones*, 1953

J Lees-Milne, *English Country Houses, Baroque 1685–1715*, 1970

S Parissien, *The Adam Style*, 1996

S Sitwell, *British Architects and Craftsmen 1600–1830*, 1948

J Summerson, *Architecture in Britain 1530–1830*, 1953 (revised 1991)

J Summerson, *Inigo Jones*, 1966

J Summerson, *Georgian London*, 1945 (revised 1988)

R Tavernor, *Palladio and Palladianism*, 1991

M Whinney, *Wren*, 1971

G Worsley, *Classical Architecture in Britain: The Heroic Age*, 1995

A Youngson, *The Making of Classical Edinburgh*, 1966

NINETEENTH AND TWENTIETH CENTURIES

C Aslet, *The Last Country Houses*, 1982

R Banham, *The New Brutalism*, 1966

J Mordaunt Crook, *The Greek Revival*, 1972

C Cunningham, *Victorian and Edwardian Town Halls*, 1991

J S Curl, *Victorian Architecture*, 1990

C Davies, *High Tech Architecture*, 1988

D Dean, *The Thirties: Recalling the English Architectural Scene*, 1983

R Dixon and S Mauthesius, *Victorian Architecture*, 1978

R Fellows, *Edwardian Architecture: Style and Society*, 1995

J Furneaux, *Victorian Architecture*, 1966

M Girouard, *The Victorian Country House*, 1971

M Girouard, *Sweetness and Light, the 'Queen Anne Movement'*, 1860–1900, 1977

J Glancey, *New British Architecture*, 1989

H S Goodhart-Rendel, *English Architecture since the Regency*, 1953

Further Reading

T Hinchcliffe, *North Oxford*, 1992

H R Hitchcock, *Architecture: Nineteenth and Twentieth Centuries*, 1971

P Howell and I Sutton, *The Faber Guide to Victorian Churches*, 1989

N Jackson, *Nineteenth Century Bath*, 1991

M Miller, *Garden Cities and Town Planning*, 1992

S Muthesius, *The English Terraced House*, 1982

S Muthesius, *The High Victorian Movement in Architecture 1850–1870*, 1972

N Pevsner, *Pioneers of Modern Design*, 1960

M H Port, *The Houses of Parliament*, 1976

E Rosenberg, *Architect's Choice, Art in Architecture in Britain since 1945*, 1994

A Service, *Edwardian Architecture*, 1977

D Watkins, *The Building of Britain: Regency*, 1982

M Weinreb, *London Architecture: Features and Facades*, 1993

F Wordsall, *Victorian City. Glasgow*, 1982

Index

Index

Index

Index

Index

Index

Index